Fundamentals of
Catholic Theology
in Just Over 100 pages

A Theological Defense of the Catholic Faith in Opposition to Protestant Defiance

PARKER MANNING

ISBN 978-1-63844-061-1 (paperback)
ISBN 978-1-63844-062-8 (digital)

Christian Faith Publishing
832 Park Avenue
Meadville, PA 16335
www.christianfaithpublishing.com

Printed in the United States of America

Special thanks to Fr. Joel Phelps, Fr. Tom Otto, Fr. Peter Pilon, and Mr. Matt Gehm

To be deep in history is to cease to be Protestant.
—Saint John Henry Newman

Contents

Introduction

I wrote this book to be informative, not argumentative. Currently, too many Catholics doubt their faith and are not aware of how strong it can really be. Too many Catholics don't understand why we do what we do and the reasons we do them: why we go to confession, why we receive communion, why we believe in Purgatory, why we believe in transubstantiation, why we believe in apostolic succession, and other questions. I wrote this book to answer those questions and many more.

I answer these questions not only for Catholics who need to have their faith rejuvenated but for those who don't agree with Catholicism because they believe the falsehoods that have been spread about the Catholic Church and faith. As Fulton Sheen said, "There are not one hundred people in the United States who hate the Catholic Church, but there are millions who hate what they wrongly perceive the Catholic Church to be."

People need to be aware of the greatness that is the Catholic Church and the philosophies that come with it. After all, if a Church was started by God, we should study the philosophies of that Church. Unfortunately, many people hate the Catholic Church because of the philosophies portrayed by those who do not know about it. I wrote this book to dismantle any doubts that Catholics have. For example, setting an example of being Catholic cannot happen if people have doubts in their faith. Becoming "truly Catholic" is something that everyone, even Protestants, should strive for. As Mother Angelica famously said, "If Catholics would rise up and be truly Catholic, the world would change overnight." In order to change the world, Catholics need to be truly Catholic. In doing so, we also become more like Jesus.

This book will help Catholics become "truly Catholic." For one, readers will lose the doubts they have in their faith. This will help those straying away from the Church and help them restore their faith in God. In doing so, they will also become better people by living like Jesus.

For the Catholic, I want to make sure they stay Catholic. For the person who is considering becoming Catholic, I want to make sure that the individual becomes Catholic. For the person who hates the Church, I hope and pray that their dislike is null and void after reading this treatise.

Catholics also need to be more aware of the philosophies they believe and why they believe those ideologies. If not, they are simply robots doing what the priest tells them to do.

If you want a more in-depth book on this, take a look at Trent Horn's *The Case for Catholicism*. Trent goes deeper into these theologies, but as the name of this book suggests, I only talk about the fundamentals.

With all that being said, there is one main reason why I wrote this book. Catholics need to be helped with doubts that they have. While having doubts is not a bad thing, these doubts need to be diminished in order to fully live with God. That is exceptionally hard to do by oneself. That's why books like these are overwhelmingly important. All in all, God bless. Those who get to the end of the book will not only become "truly Catholic"; they'll also learn something as well. They'll also be able to understand and appreciate their faith much more.

One Holy, Apostolic, Authoritative, and Infallible Church

Before I begin to talk about the history of the Church, I first need to discuss some things. First, Jesus would have had to create a church. The nondenominational argument "Jesus didn't create a religion; he just wants you to have a relationship with him" doesn't make sense. At this time, there was no such thing as the Bible. So, you would need a Church official to determine objectively which books should be in the Bible and which books shouldn't be. Many Protestants will argue that the books in the Bible are "self-revealing". But if they were self-revealing, why was there a massive debate about them? Then after the Bible was compiled by that group, they would need to tell people what the verses meant. The Bible was not meant to be given to different groups of people so that they all have different opinions on who Jesus was.[1] It is a book with objective meanings. You need a Church to establish what those meanings are. That same Church would also make rulings for the Christian people. A Church started and inspired by God Himself would have the authority to determine how Christians should live as well. That being said, that church would be one created at the time of Jesus, and not one 1,500 years later. This infallibility is what makes the Catholic Church so much more special than any Protestant one.

One cannot possibly talk about the history of the Church without first discussing the history of its most important object, the Bible. Firstly, the Bible was not officially compiled until a few centu-

---

[1] 2 Peter 1:20

ries later.[2] This fact is especially important in the book of Acts when the Bereans are checking Paul's word to see if it matches Scripture. They would have only had the Old Testament. Moreover, even if they had the entire Bible at their disposal, attempting to refute Paul by saying "the Bible says this" would be rather doltish, as Saint Paul would know much more than the Bereans on what the Bible says. If there is an argument, Paul would've certainly corrected them.

This creates an issue for those who believe in *sola scriptura* (Scripture alone). The Bible certainly could have changed slightly through those years before it was written down. It's worth noting that the *sola scriptura* argument is not "everything that Jesus and the apostles said is in Scripture." However, their philosophy of "nothing else is inspired by God besides the Bible" is an unbiblical idea.

Sola scriptura is something that is highly debated among Protestants and Catholics—that is, the argument over whether Scripture is the ultimate or only element regarding infallible doctrine. There are several arguments that are brought up by Protestants to testify that Scripture alone is biblical.

The most well-known verse would be 2 Timothy 3:16 where Saint Paul tells Timothy that all Scripture is God-breathed ($\theta\varepsilon\acute{o}\pi\nu\varepsilon\upsilon\sigma\tau o\varsigma$). This argument has limited significance for theological purposes. Just because Scripture is God-breathed does not mean that other things cannot be God-breathed. Citing this verse from the Protestant side is rather ridiculous. Take an example from today's world. If I were to say that all sodas have carbonation, it would be absurd for someone to hear that and think "the only thing that has carbonation is a soda." This is rather simplistic, and it shouldn't even be debated from the Protestant side. Just because Scripture is God-breathed does not mean that that is the only thing that is God-breathed.[3] Not only that, but this is a very clear circular-reasoning fallacy. They believe the Bible is inspired because the Bible says it is inspired. Where do these books come from?

---

[2] History.com Editors, "The Bible," History.com. A&E Television Networks, January 19, 2018.

[3] It is worth noting that Catholics are allowed to believe that only Scripture is God-breathed. However, one must believe that Tradition and the Magisterium are both infallible.

Along with that, who gets to decide which books are Scripture and which books are not? Again, there is no objectivity without a Church.

Another verse that Protestants will cite is 1 John 2:27, when he says that the Parthians do not need anyone to teach them because there is an anointing within them. Immediately, this verse seems like a weird one to cite. If John really meant that Christians need no one to teach them, he would be contradicting himself. "You do not need anyone to teach you" is a teaching in itself. Also, nearly every Protestant Church has some sort of analysis of a specific Bible reading during the church service by the pastor and Sunday school for the little ones. If they put their money where their mouth was when it comes to this verse in the first epistle of John, they'd do away with both of those things.

However, the philosophy that Christians don't need a priest to tell them what the Bible says because the Holy Spirit will guide them is somehow gaining substance. The only reality in which this argument makes any sense would be one where all Christian theology is nonpartisan. Clearly, this is not the case. If the Holy Spirit is the only thing necessary, then subjectivity shouldn't exist. Therefore, we need more than just our own interpretation. The alternative would either be a Holy Spirit that only interprets the Bible for some (needless today, one would have a hard time arguing that the Holy Spirit interprets the Bible for their church and not the church down the street) or one that lies to certain individuals about what God's word entails. Because neither of these scenarios make sense, it's reasonable to assume that Christians are called to use more than just their own interpretation of the Bible. Now this isn't to say that the Holy Spirit isn't enough by itself. It just means that as fallible humans, we need help following God. It is not the Holy Spirit that needs assistance following us. Rather, it is us that needs assistance following the Holy Spirit.

Within the Catholic view of Sacred Tradition, there are a few distinctions that must be made. Integral Tradition is the preaching of the Apostles before Scripture. Then after the New Testament is written and the Apostles are dead, we have inherent Tradition (the interpretation of Scripture that is explicit in Scripture), declarative Tradition (Tradition that is implicit in Scripture. Remember, the Church has to declare these things.) Then there is also a concept known as constitutive Tradition, which is the idea that there is Tradition that is not explicit or implicit in Scripture. As someone who holds to material sufficiency, I reject this view.

To recap, the Catholic view of Sacred Tradition is this:

Scripture- Infallible; what is being interpreted

Tradition- The interpretation of said Scripture, comes in when Scripture is not clear (not including the idea of constitutive Tradition)

Magisterium-The interpreter of Scripture, comes in when Scripture and Tradition are both ambiguous

Setting aside theology, even from a logical perspective, Sola Scriptura makes little sense. Let's say for instance the Protestants are right and there is no infallible interpreter on Earth today. This would essentially mean that Jesus (in His infinite wisdom) told us things like "If you blaspheme the Holy Spirit you will never be forgiven"[4] and "Unless you are born of water and the Spirit, you cannot enter the kingdom of God"[5]. Both are very ambiguous statements with very extreme connotations. (It's worth noting that what these verses mean are disagreed upon in Protestant circles.) What are we to make of this? Are we to conclude that Jesus made these statements without clarification and encouraged us to figure it out on our own? And if we were wrong, send us to an eternal torment? Nonsense, Jesus would have done no such thing. Sola Scriptura, simply put, is a doctrine of men fabricated by Luther and believed by no one else before him.

Some Protestants have tried arguing that it is the authors of the books in the Bible that determine canon. This is not true. You would need a third party, because not just anyone can write a book, put it in the Bible, and still call it the Word of God. Even if every book in the Bible claimed to be the Word of God, it would be a circular argument to conclude that these books are inspired by God. Essentially, you are arguing that these books are inspired because they claim inspiration. The Catholic Church has the authority to decide these things. Not some random philosopher living in the sixteenth century.

---

[4] Mark 3:28-29, Matthew 12:31
[5] John 3:5

I also should bring up the history of the Bible itself, because the Catholic Bible and the Protestant "Bible" have very different histories. Notice how I put Protestant "Bible" in quotes. This is because contrary to popular belief, Protestants do not read the real Bible. Their "Bible" is merely a translated version of some of the books in the real Bible. There have been four separate Catholic councils of bishops that have confirmed that the Catholic Bible has the books that are inspired by God. These were the Council of Rome in AD 382, the Council of Hippo in AD 393, the Council of Carthage in AD 397, and the Second Council of Carthage in AD 419. If the Church dictated canon, it would be rather preposterous for them to add books that directly contradict the teachings of the Church. If the Church so vehemently misinterprets the Bible, to a point where it is astonishingly obvious, as Protestants will say, why would they even put those books as canon? Why not discard them? Martin Luther took out seven books in the Bible, also known as the deuterocanonical books. This is a major reason that my family is no longer Protestant. Who is he to decide which books should be in the Bible and which ones shouldn't? Moreover, if Luther took books out, then the Protestant "Bible" is not truly the Bible.[6] If someone were to take the Bible but rip out the book of Matthew, then it would no longer be the Bible. This philosophy works with any other book as well. So since the Protestant "Bible" does not have all of the books, it's not really the Bible. Catholics can trace their Bible back to the times of Jesus, whereas Protestants cannot. If someone is Protestant, that individual is trusting the opinion of the specific theologian who branched off to create a specific religion, rather than Jesus Christ. Protestants have a multitude of excuses as to why it was righteous to remove these books, saying that we aren't sure where they came from, the Jews rejected them, and there are supposed errors throughout. Even Jerome originally rejected the Deuterocanonicals! There are several things wrong with this way of thinking.

---

6   It's worth noting that Luther did not exactly remove books, but he did do things that led others to remove them.

- We aren't aware of the authors of many of the books in the Bible, meaning we aren't sure exactly where they came from. Shall we throw out those books too?
- Even if the Jews rejected them, it does not mean they are not inspired by God. After all, the Jews reject all of the New Testament. Is the New Testament not inspired by God because the Jews rejected it?
- The "supposed errors" argument intrigues me the most out of them all. The Bible is a book of many supposed errors. The deuterocanonical books are no different.

  o Even if one did find an error in those books, you would have to first explain why it is an actual error and not an apparent error.
  o Then you would have to find an actual error in each of the seven books (and those additional parts of Daniel and Esther). It would rather be ridiculous to cite an actual error in 1 Maccabees and throw out Tobit as a result.

- Finally, Jerome and other Church fathers after him origi- nally did not view the Deuterocanonical as divine. However, they also submitted to the authority of the Church. Jerome was a Catholic priest, after all. It would stand to reason that Jerome, like many others, accepted them after the Church accepted them."[7]

  o These books were unanimously looked upon as Scripture in the early church until Jerome (who changed his mind), so it would be preposterous to reject them as Scripture when there is far less attesta- tion for books like Esther and Revelation. In fact, if these books are not Scripture, this is the best that an

---

[7] Marshall, D., "Did St Jerome reject the Deuterocanonical books?" October 1, 2011, retrieved January 29, 2021.

honest Protestant could say regarding the early church. They were unanimously attested to until about 400 AD, then that man later changed his mind. How preposterous would it be if the Gospel of Thomas and Judas were unanimously attested to as Scripture until 400 by a man who changed his mind? If the Protestant canon is true, that is just the case.

o   Because of this information, we can conclude that the Protestant canon makes very little sense historically. They accept a book like Hebrews that was heavily contested in the early church but reject a book like Baruch that was unanimously accepted. They will also accept a book like Protestant Esther that does not talk about God, but will reject a book like Wisdom of Solomon that has an explicit articulation of Jesus' relationship with the Father along with His crucifixion.[8] The author of Hebrews also calls the Maccabees biblical characters in Hebrews 11:35,[9] which raises another problem for Protestants.

The verses in the Bible that seem to nullify tradition hold little ground theologically because they're too ambiguous to be argued convincingly. For example, when Paul tells the Corinthians to not go beyond what is written,[10] it doesn't make sense to use that as a message to all Christians for several reasons. First and foremost, if Paul was saying "Don't go beyond what is written" as to say "Don't go beyond the word of God in Scripture," it's important to remember that the Corinthians would have only had access to the two letters that they had received from Paul. Obviously, the knowledge of Jesus exists outside those two letters. In a literal sense, Paul saying "do not go beyond what is written in Scripture" to the Corinthians would be the same thing as "Do not read any other books in the Bible or listen to any apostles." Not only

---

8   For more on this, check out "The Case for the Deuterocanon" by Gary Michuta

9   "Take the Apocrypha Apocalypse Challenge!" *YouTube*, 13 Nov 2020, https://youtu.be/T78xT71v0Io.

10 1 Corinthians 4:6

that, but Paul would not tell the Corinthians to not go beyond what is written in the entire Bible because the Bible had not been compiled yet.

But let's say for argument's sake that someone is arguing that Paul meant all books of the Bible when he said "Do not go beyond what is written."

First and foremost, we don't know if Paul was even referring to Scripture in this verse. There's much ambiguity among biblical scholars over what Paul meant. However, the argument that Saint Paul is advocating for *sola scriptura* in this verse is easily refuted, since he would be contradicting himself in his first letter to the Corinthians: "I praise you for remembering me in everything and for holding to the traditions just as I passed them on to you."[11]

Saint Paul also instructs the Thessalonians to hold on to traditions: "So then, brothers and sisters, stand firm and hold fast to the teachings we passed on to you, whether by word of mouth or by letter."[12] Later in this same letter, he instructs the Thessalonians to shun those not acting according to tradition: "In the name of the Lord Jesus Christ, we command you, brothers and sisters, to keep away from every believer who is idle and disruptive and does not live according to the teaching you received from us."[13]

Saint Paul insists that believers must not only believe, but live according to the teaching received from the apostles.

To argue against this, Protestants say that Jesus spoke against traditions in the Bible.[14] However, this is not exactly accurate. These people were ignoring the Word of God for traditions not passed down by Him. This is much different from a Catholic who holds true to the traditions of Jesus Christ and the apostles.

In fact, Protestants rely on tradition whether they admit it or not. For instance, outside the Gospel of John, none of the other gospels reveal the names of the author. This actually goes for most books in the Bible. Regardless, Protestants would need to use tradition to help them know who wrote those books in the Bible where the author is not explicitly

---

[11] 1 Corinthians 11:2
[12] 2 Thessalonians 2:15
[13] 2 Thessalonians 3:6
[14] Mark 7:9; Matthew 15:3

stated. The surrogate would be the same as admitting some books of the Bible could have been written by people who were not inspired by God. In that case, we would be compelled to throw those books of the Bible.

A Church founded on the apostles makes sense. Firstly, Jesus delegated specific men to be His apostles. In the Gospel of John, Jesus says to the apostles, "You did not choose me, but I chose you and appointed you so that you might go and bear fruit—fruit that will last—and so that whatever you ask in my name the Father will give you."[15] These would be men qualified to spread the Gospel. In fact, Jesus instructs them to do this in the Gospel of John: "Peace be with you! As the Father has sent me, I am sending you."[16] Saint Paul also tells us in his letter to the Ephesians that the apostles were equipped to spread the Word of God. He writes, "So Christ himself gave the apostles, the prophets, the evangelists, the pastors and teachers, to equip his people for works of service, so that the body of Christ may be built up."[17]

In the book of Ephesians, Saint Paul says that the Church was built on apostles: "Built on the foundation of the apostles and prophets, with Christ Jesus himself as the chief cornerstone."[18] Finally, in the Gospel of Matthew, Jesus says that He wants to give His power to the apostles: "Then Jesus came to them and said, 'All authority in Heaven and on earth has been given to me. Therefore go and make disciples of all nations, baptizing them in the name of the Father and of the Son and of the Holy Spirit, and teaching them to obey everything I have commanded you.'"[19]

Jesus also put Peter in charge of His Church:

"And I tell you that you are Peter, and on this rock I will build my Church, and the gates of Hades will not overcome it. I will give you the keys of the kingdom of Heaven; whatever you bind on earth will be bound in Heaven, and whatever you loose on earth will be loosed in Heaven."[20]

---

[15] John 15:16
[16] John 20:21
[17] Ephesians 4:11–12
[18] Ephesians 2:20
[19] Matthew 28:18–20
[20] Matthew 16:18

The most prevalent response to this is that if Jesus was speaking Greek, He uses two different words for "Peter" and "rock" (Petros versus Petra). There are a couple of problems with this assertion. Firstly, Jesus most likely spoke Aramaic, a dead language. Many scholars believe this to be the case because during the time, this was the most common language in the area.[21] If Jesus is speaking Aramaic, this argument doesn't stand any ground. Rock is *kêfâ* no matter how it is used. So, Jesus would have most likely said, "You are Peter (*kêfâ*) and on this (*kêfâ*) I will build my Church."[22]

But let's assume for a second that Jesus was speaking Greek. Does the different vowel mean that Peter was not the rock on which Jesus would build His Church? Keep in mind that the two words do not mean different things. Rather, it is the male and female version of the same word, rock. Moreover, if Jesus had called Peter "Petra" this wouldn't make sense, as Peter is male (*Petra* is female). Since rock is a feminine noun in Greek, it would be linguistically inaccurate to call Peter "*Petra*." Matthew makes this distinction for us for that reason. In order for someone to say that Jesus was talking about two completely different things because of one vowel change would take some extreme linguistic gymnastics. We can prove this because when the word "rock" is mentioned in Greek and it doesn't refer to Peter, it is always *Petra* (or a variation thereof). Luke 8:13 is just one example of this.

The most common exegesis that Protestants will have regarding these verses is that it is not Peter that is the rock, but the confession of faith that Peter makes. Without much thought, this analysis raises a couple of questions:

1. Why would Jesus change Simon's name to Rock if he were not the rock? If that were the case, Matthew 16:18 would be read like this: "You are now Rock, and upon this rock, I

---

[21] S. Pruitt (2020, March 30), "What Language Did Jesus Speak?" Retrieved August 28, 2020.

[22] Be advised that Catholics are allowed to believe that Peter is the rock, that Jesus is the rock, and that Peter's faith is the rock. The Church has not defined that Peter is the rock, but have merely defined that Jesus is establishing the papacy in this verse.

will build my Church, but you are not the rock on which I will build my church." If you needed to read that quote a few times, you aren't alone. But that is essentially what Jesus would be saying if Peter was not the rock.

2.   Why did Jesus give Peter the keys in the very next verse? "I will give you the keys of the kingdom of heaven; whatever you bind on earth will be bound in heaven, and whatever you loose on earth will be loosed in heaven." If Jesus is talking about Peter's confession of faith, the message He is trying to convey becomes even more confusing than in the previous example. It essentially goes, "You are now Rock, and upon this rock I will build my Church, but you are not the rock on which I will build my church. The rock on which I will build my church is your confession of faith. I will give you the keys..." Why is Peter the one receiving the keys if it was just the confession of faith that was the rock? You could say that Jesus is speaking to all of us and not just Peter, but that would be a rather large assumption considering Jesus and Peter were alone at this moment.

Still not convinced? Even Gerhard Kittel's *Theological Greek Dictionary of the New Testament* admits that the rock in Matthew 16:18 is referring to Peter:

> The obvious pun that has made its way into the Greek text...suggests a material identity between petra and Petros...as it is impossible to differentiate strictly between the two words...Petros himself is this petra, not just his faith or his confession...
>
> The idea of the Reformers that he is referring to the faith of Peter is quite inconceivable... For there is no reference here to the faith of Peter. Rather, the parallelism of "thou art Rock" and "on this rock I will build" shows that the second rock can only be the same as the first.

It is thus evident that Jesus is referring to Peter, to whom he has given the name Rock… To this extent Roman Catholic exegesis is right and all Protestant attempts to evade this interpretation are to be rejected.

Rather surprising to me, the consensus among Protestant commentators today is that rock indeed refers to Peter himself, not his faith. They will then argue against any sort of succession of this power. But nonetheless, they will admit that Jesus is talking about Peter here, not just his confession of faith.[23]

As seen by this verse, Jesus not only created a church, but made Peter the head of it. Saint Paul also refers to Peter as Cephas (rock) in his letter to the Galatians.[24]

Jesus also instructs us to be one flock with one shepherd. In the Gospel of John, he says, "I have other sheep that are not of this sheep pen. I must bring them also. They too will listen to my voice, and there shall be one flock and one shepherd."[25]

We are obviously the flock in this sense. But the question then remains: Who is the shepherd? Jesus tells later in that same gospel that it is Peter. He tells Peter to feed his sheep,[26] meaning he would be the ultimate shepherd. Some will combat this by saying that we are all shepherds because we should all teach and guide those to the faith. This is true, in a sense. We should all shepherd people to the faith. But Peter has a unique role. We see this later in the Gospel of Luke:

"Simon, Simon, Satan has asked to sift all of you as wheat. But I have prayed for you, Simon, that your faith may not fail. And when you have turned back, strengthen your brothers."[27]

[23.] Armstrong, D., "Peter the ROCK: Protestant Contra-Catholic Exegetical bias," April 19, 2017, retrieved February 11, 2021.

[24] Galatians 1:18

[25] John 10:16

[26] John 21:17

[27] Luke 22:31

Here, we see Jesus giving a direct prayer to Peter so that he may strengthen his brothers (the apostles). Why do this specifically to Simon Peter unless he is going to lead Christ's Church?

Peter is also the leader of the apostles. This is seen all throughout the book of Acts when Peter is leading the preaching. Therefore, it would make sense that Jesus would have given power to Peter over anyone else.

For one, he was the head of the meeting in the book of Acts:

> When they arrived, they went upstairs to the room where they were staying. Those present were Peter, John, James and Andrew; Philip and Thomas, Bartholomew and Matthew; James son of Alphaeus and Simon the Zealot, and Judas son of James. They all joined together constantly in prayer, along with the women and Mary the mother of Jesus, and with his brothers. In those days Peter stood up among the believers (a group numbering about a hundred and twenty) and said, "Brothers and sisters, the Scripture had to be fulfilled in which the Holy Spirit spoke long ago through David concerning Judas, who served as guide for those who arrested Jesus. He was one of our number and shared in our ministry." (With the payment he received for his wickedness, Judas bought a field; there he fell headlong, his body burst open and all his intestines spilled out. Everyone in Jerusalem heard about this, so they called that field in their language Akeldama, that is, Field of Blood.) "For," said Peter, "it is written in the Book of Psalms:
>
> May his place be deserted; let there be no one to dwell in it, and may another take his place of leadership. Therefore it is necessary to choose one of the men who have been with us the whole time the Lord Jesus was living among us, beginning from John's Baptism to the time when Jesus

was taken up from us. For one of these must become a witness with us of his resurrection."[28]

While this does not prove that Peter was the first pope, it does prove that Peter was the leader among the apostles after Jesus had ascended into Heaven.

He was also the leader of the first council in Jerusalem:

"After much discussion, Peter got up and addressed them: 'Brothers, you know that some time ago God made a choice among you that the Gentiles might hear from my lips the message of the gospel and believe.'"[29]

As shown by the verse, Peter addressed the group. This would imply that he was the leader. He even goes as far as to say that God made a choice among them for Peter to be the leader in preaching.

Protestants will argue that it was actually James who led the council for a couple of reasons. First, they will cite James when he says "listen to me" later in the book of Acts.[30] This point is easily refuted, seeing that shouting "listen" in a meeting does not always constitute superiority. Furthermore, it is Peter who speaks first during the meeting—not James. The person who speaks first during meetings is always the one with prestige.

However, the point that really hits home for Catholic theology is that it is Peter, not James, who makes the decision first. I cite this in the previous page. Peter says that God made a choice among them, and that choice was Peter. The next few verses after Acts 15:7 illustrate this:

> God, who knows the heart, showed that he accepted them by giving the Holy Spirit to them, just as he did to us. He did not discriminate between us and them, for he purified their hearts by faith. Now then, why do you try to test God by putting on the necks of Gentiles a yoke that

---

[28] Acts 1:13–22
[29] Acts 15:7
[30] Acts 15:13

neither we nor our ancestors have been able to
bear? No! We believe it is through the grace of
our Lord Jesus that we are saved, just as they are.[31]

The philosophy regarding salvation is not argued. Doctrinally, Peter
makes clear where salvation comes. When James says "Listen to me," he
does this after Peter makes the final decision. James is also only making
a suggestion, whereas Peter is saying definitive doctrine in those quotes
before James makes the suggestion (again, not an emphatic command).

Be that as it may, it would be rather unexpected that James was
the leader of the council after Peter spoke first, and settles the debate
in Acts 15:6. Furthermore, James speaks in a suggestive manner after
Peter makes the final infallible decision.

Peter also received the first converts, performed the first mira-
cle after Pentecost,[32] inflicted the first punishment,[33] and excommu-
nicated the first heretic.[34] When the apostles are listed by name, Peter
is always first.[35] This most likely is in order of primacy and not some
other reason, since Judas is also always listed last (for instance, if it
was by age, as some Protestants have argued, then John would have
been last in order). The Bible also refers to the apostles as "Peter and
his companions" a couple of times.[36] He also speaks for the apostles in
several instances.[37] Lastly, Peter's name occurs 195 times in the Bible.
This is more than the rest combined. It can be inferred that Peter was
the leader of the Apostles. As many have said already, the doctrine of
the papacy is far from the most important doctrine. However, if Jesus
wants a pope for His Church and only one Church has a pope, we
should all be members of that Church. This does not, however, mean
that Peter was perfect. Protestants like to use Saint Paul's outing of
Peter for his hypocrisy in Galatians 2:11–14 as evidence that he was

---

[31] Acts 15:8–11
[32] Acts 3:6–7
[33] Acts 5:1–11
[34] Acts 8:21
[35] Matthew 10:1–4; Mark 3:16–19; Luke 6:14–16; Acts 1:13
[36] Luke 9:32, Mark 16:7
[37] Matthew 18:21; Mark 8:29; Luke 8:45; Luke 12:41; John 6:69

not the pope. There are a couple of things wrong with this. Number one, Saint Paul still refers to Peter as Cephas (rock), so he still believes that Peter is the rock that Christ was referring to in Matthew 16:18. Additionally, just because a pope or other church leader is hypocritical or does something sinful does not refute his authority. It just means that he is a human being with free will and the ability to choose evil. Since those authoritative powers were only given to the Catholic Church, there should only be one flock to Christ's shepherd. Instead, there are hundreds of Protestant denominations. This is not what Christ would have wanted. Since Jesus created the Catholic Church and calls us to be one,[38] it would stand to reason that everyone should be Catholic. Why do something that is contradictory to what Jesus taught?

You also see Jesus talking about authority of the Church in Matthew's Gospel: "If your brother or sister sins, go and point out their fault just between the two of you. If they listen to you, you have won them over. But if they will not listen, take one or two others along so that every matter may be established by the testimony of two or three witnesses. If they still refuse to listen, tell it to the Church, and if they refuse to listen even to the Church, treat them as you would a pagan or a tax collector."[39]

Moreover, if this is the Church instituted by Christ and guided by the Holy Spirit,[40] it is infallible. Some Protestant theologians will go the opposite way with this. They'll say, "Since the Church is fallible, Jesus did not create it." In order to make this argument, one would have to show a fallible mistake the Church has made that contradicts the Bible. However, how do Protestants judge this? If Protestants attempt to argue that nothing outside Scripture is infallible, then the Bible is not infallible. If the authors who wrote the Bible were not infallible, then they could not have possibly written an infallible book. Therefore, outside the Bible, infallible things exist. The argument that the Catholic Church is not infallible because of a

---

[38] Romans 16:17
[39] Matthew 18:15-20
[40] John 16:13

Protestant's subjective view of what the Bible says is a direct contra-diction to what Saint Peter teaches in 2 Peter 1:20.

Instead, we need to look at church history and determine whether a church was instituted by Christ. Along with this, we need to determine what church that is and if it has changed teaching over time. If a church has fit all those parameters, it would be crazy to not be a part of it. As I've proven through various Bible verses, this Church is the Catholic Church.

Even though we can without a doubt prove that the Catholic Church was instituted by Christ, there are some Catholic philosophies that are not explicitly taught in the Bible. Therefore, we should look at early Christian writings and read what they wrote about specific top-ics. It's important to know that the early Church Fathers did mildly disagree on some subjects. When talking about Church Fathers who disagreed, we first have to recognize different types of disagreement. Some are only apparent disagreements. For example, one can say that Chicago is to the south, but I say it is to the north. Both of these statements can be true even if they sound contradictory because we can live in different places. But some are truly differences of fact. For example, someone says two plus two is four, and another two plus two is five. Only in this last case is there a problem. If you ask a Protestant, "Why do the Gospels disagree with each other?" they would probably be able to explain this; there are only apparent disagreements.

However, it is true that sometimes the Church Fathers disagreed in fact and not only in appearance. With this being said, the question "Why do the Church Fathers disagree?" is a loaded one. It assumes in this question that it is a problem if the Church Fathers disagree. It assumes that the Catholic Church believes that the Church Fathers always agree about everything. We do not. Any individual Church Father is just a fallible human being. They can make mistakes and be wrong, and that is totally fine.

However, there are several things that are unanimously attested to by the early Church Fathers, and I will be dictating those through-out the book.

Objection 1: Just because it is unanimously attested to does not mean it is true

Reply to Objection 1: Yes it does. Setting aside other problems that this poses for Protestants (which I develop further in my book *Catholic God, True God)*, I'm not sure how this even happens. Baptismal Regeneration is something that is overwhelmingly (and unanimously) attested to by the early Church Fathers. Let's imagine for a second that Baptismal Regeneration is not Orthodox—Baptism does not actually save. We would assume that Jesus taught it to His Apostles, then His Apostles taught it, then...what? Did their disciples just choose not to listen? Did they refuse to read the Scripture that they revered so much? Were they influenced by someone? What happened? If this sounds ridiculous, it is.

Objection 2: These things are not unanimous

Reply to Objection 2: I would encourage anyone to give me a father who taught differently

Objection 3: Not all Church Fathers wrote about a specific topic

Reply to Objection 3: This is true, but it is not what I mean by unanimous. What I mean is that it is overwhelmingly attested to, and no one seems to argue against it.

Objection 4: Writings from the true Christians were destroyed

Reply to Objection 4: This argument cannot possibly be taken seriously, as it is the ultimate argument from silence and has no historical backing.

Another thing to think about—if these fathers were so overwhelmingly wrong on things like Baptismal Regeneration and justification, how could they have possibly gotten the 27 book New Testament correct?

So what does the Church actually believe about the Church Fathers and Sacred Tradition? We believe that we can look at them as a whole to see the true faith. Because of this, it is appropriate that some individual Church Fathers disagree. Their teaching is just a general guide—it is usually a trustworthy guide, but everything they say is not infallible. Again, this is why we need someone who can make a final say when there is a disagreement (i.e., the Catholic Church).

While it doesn't matter when the Church Fathers disagree, we should at least be mindful as to what they have to say. After all, these men would have been alive only a few generations after Jesus and the apostles. Think of it as the childhood game of telephone. For those unfamiliar, it's a game played by kids where you sit in a line, and the first person whispers a message to the next, then the next person whispers that message to the next, and so on. The way that game is generally played, the message gets more distorted the later it gets in the line.

This is the same with Church Fathers. Since they were alive right after the time of Jesus (beginning of the line), the chance that their message is the one Jesus taught is much more likely than someone like Martin Luther, who lived around 1,500 years after Jesus died.

If we are to be one, we need to have a leader to be able to confirm or deny doctrine. Peter's primacy and the origins of him as pope are clearly referenced by early Church Fathers and the successors that came after him. In AD 170, Tatian the Syrian, an early philosophical writer, wrote,

> Simon Cephas answered and said, "You are the Messiah, the Son of the living God." Jesus answered and said unto him, "Blessed are you, Simon, son of Jonah: flesh and blood has not revealed it unto thee, but my Father which is in Heaven. And I say unto thee also, that you are Cephas, and on this rock will I build my Church; and the gates of Hades shall not prevail against it."[41]

Here, Tatian is saying that Peter is Christ's "rock" and that the gates of Hades (Hell) shouldn't prevail against it.

Here's another quote from Tertullian who was referenced earlier. In AD 200, he wrote:

> Was anything withheld from the knowledge of Peter, who is called "the rock on which the Church would be built" [Matt. 16:18] with the power of "loosing and binding in Heaven and on earth" [Matt. 16:19]?[42] [T]he Lord said to Peter,

---

[41] *The Diatesseron* 23 [A.D. 170]
[42] *Demurrer Against the Heretics* 22 [A.D. 200]

"On this rock I will build my Church, I have given you the keys of the kingdom of Heaven [and] whatever you shall have bound or loosed on earth will be bound or loosed in Heaven" [Matt. 16:18–19]… What kind of man are you, subverting and changing what was the manifest intent of the Lord when he conferred this personally upon Peter? Upon *you*, he says, I will build my Church; and I will give to *you* the keys.[43]

Here, Tertullian is referring to the same Bible verses that Tatian the Syrian was referring to earlier, Matthew 16:18–19. Peter was Christ's rock, and upon that rock he built his Church.

Here's a quote from Clement's letter to Saint James. It says, "Be it known to you, my Lord, that Simon [Peter], who, for the sake of the true faith, and the most sure foundation of his doctrine, was set apart to be the foundation of the Church, and for this end was by Jesus himself, with his truthful mouth, named Peter."

Here, the authors of the letter are saying that Peter is "the foundation of the Church." Could this mean that he was just the leader? Possibly, but if one man was pope, it would have been the leader, correct?

Here's a quote from an early pope, Pope Damasus I. In 382 he wrote:

Likewise it is decreed… that it ought to be announced that… the holy Roman Church has been placed at the forefront not by the conciliar decisions of other Churches, but has received the primacy by the evangelic voice of our Lord and Savior, who says: "You are Peter, and upon this rock I will build my Church, and the gates of Hell will not prevail against it; and I will give to you the keys of the kingdom of Heaven…" [Matt. 16:18–19]. The first see, therefore, is that of Peter

---

[43] *Modesty* 21:9–10 [A.D. 220]

FUNDAMENTALS OF CATHOLIC THEOLOGY
IN JUST OVER 100 PAGES

the apostle, that of the Roman Church, which has neither stain nor blemish nor anything like it.[44]

This is a quote from a very early pope that's saying that Peter was the first pope.

Here's another quote from another pope. In 408, Pope Innocent I wrote,

> In seeking the things of God… you have acknowledged that judgment is to be referred to us [the pope], and have shown that you know that is owed to the Apostolic See [Rome], if all of us placed in this position are to desire to follow the apostle himself [Peter] from whom the episcopate itself and the total authority of this name have emerged.[45]

This shows not only that Peter was the first pope, but those authoritative powers were eventually given to Pope Innocent through succession. This is yet another example of Peter's primacy among other apostles.

Apostolic succession is a core belief among Catholics, and rejected by almost every Protestant. Here's a quote from another early Pope, Pope Clement I regarding apostolic succession. In AD 80, he wrote,

> Through countryside and city [the Apostles] preached, and they appointed their earliest converts, testing them by the Spirit, to be the bishops and deacons of future believers. Nor was this a novelty, for bishops and deacons had been written about a long time earlier… Our Apostles knew through our Lord Jesus Christ that there would be strife for the office of bishop. For this reason,

---

44 *Decree of Damasus* 3 [A.D. 382]
45 *Letters* 29:1 [A.D. 408]

therefore, having received perfect foreknowledge, they appointed those who have already been mentioned and afterwards added the further provision that, if they should die, other approved men should succeed to their ministry.[46]

This is a man who, only fifty years after Jesus died, is talking about apostolic succession in its reality and purpose.

Here's a quote from Saint Jerome. In 396 he wrote, "Far be it from me to speak adversely of any of these clergy who, in succession from the apostles, confect by their sacred word the Body of Christ and through whose efforts also it is that we are Christians."

Saint Jerome, without fail, is talking about the succession of the apostles in this quote.

Here's a quote from Cyprian of Carthage. In 253 he wrote,

[T]he Church is one, and as she is one, cannot be both within and without. For if she is with [the heretic] Novatian, she was not with [Pope] Cornelius. But if she was with Cornelius, who succeeded the bishop [of Rome], Fabian, by lawful ordination, and whom, beside the honor of the priesthood the Lord glorified also with martyrdom, Novatian is not in the Church; nor can he be reckoned as a bishop, who, succeeding to no one, and despising the evangelical and apostolic tradition, sprang from himself. For he who has not been ordained in the Church can neither have nor hold to the Church in any way.[47]

Again, Cyprian is talking of apostolic succession and its reality. If all these early Christians believed in apostolic succession, it is something that we should abide by. Since apostolic succession is true,

[46] *Letter to the Corinthians* 42:4–5, 44:1–3 [A.D. 80]
[47] *Letters* 69[75]:3 [AD 253]

our teaching and practices (tradition) came directly from the apostles. Here's what early Church Fathers had to say about apostolic tradition.

Here's a quote from Irenaeus in AD 189 regarding tradition of the apostles:

> As I said before, the Church, having received this preaching and this faith, although she is disseminated throughout the whole world, yet guarded it, as if she occupied but one house. She likewise believes these things just as if she had but one soul and one and the same heart; and harmoniously she proclaims them and teaches them and hands them down, as if she possessed but one mouth. For, while the languages of the world are diverse, nevertheless, the authority of the tradition is one and the same.[48] That is why it is surely necessary to avoid them [heretics], while cherishing with the utmost diligence the things pertaining to the Church, and to lay hold of the tradition of truth... What if the Apostles had not in fact left writings to us? Would it not be necessary to follow the order of tradition, which was handed down to those to whom they entrusted the Churches? It is possible, then, for everyone in every Church, who may wish to know the truth, to contemplate the tradition of the Apostles which has been made known throughout the whole world. And we are in a position to enumerate those who were instituted bishops by the Apostles and their successors to our own times—men who neither knew nor taught anything like these heretics rave about... But since it would be too long to enumerate in such a volume as this the successions of all the Churches, we shall confound all those who, in whatever manner, whether through self-satisfac-

---

[48] *Against Heresies* 1:10:2 [AD 189]

tion or vainglory, or through blindness and wicked opinion, assemble other than where it is proper, by pointing out here the successions of the bishops of the greatest and most ancient Church known to all, founded and organized at Rome by the two most glorious Apostles, Peter and St. Paul, that Church which has the tradition and the faith which comes down to us after having been announced to men by the Apostles. With this Church, because of its superior origin, all Churches must agree—that is, all the faithful in the whole world—and it is in her that the faithful everywhere have maintained the apostolic tradition.[49]

As you can see, Irenaeus is saying that the authority of tradition is vitally important. He also makes clear that we should be members of that traditional Church.

Here's another quote from Clement of Alexandria regarding tradition from the apostles:

Well, they preserving the tradition of the blessed doctrine derived directly from the holy Apostles, Peter, James, John, and St. Paul, the sons receiving it from the father (but few were like the fathers), came by God's will to us also to deposit those ancestral and apostolic seeds. And well I know that they will exult; I do not mean delighted with this tribute, but solely on account of the preservation of the truth, according as they delivered it. For such a sketch as this, will, I think, be agreeable to a soul desirous of preserving from loss the blessed tradition.[50]

---

[49] *Against Heresies* 3:3:1 [AD 189]
[50] *Miscellanies* 1:1 [AD 208]

Here's a quote from Origen in AD 225:

> Although there are many who believe that they themselves hold to the teachings of Christ, there are yet some among them who think differently from their predecessors. The teaching of the Church has indeed been handed down through an order of succession from the Apostles and remains in the Churches even to the present time. That alone is to be believed as the truth which is in no way at variance with ecclesiastical and apostolic tradition.[51]

As Origen makes clear, we need to think like the apostles did and hold on to their traditions.

Lastly, here is the last quote from Epiphanius of Salamis regarding apostolic tradition: "It is needful also to make use of tradition, for not everything can be gotten from sacred Scripture. The holy apostles handed down some things in the scriptures, other things in tradition."[52]

I put this quote last because it is the one most comprehensible. He clearly says that we need to make use of tradition because not everything taught was in Scripture.

This would give the Church authoritative powers. If they know what the apostles taught, we need to listen to them. With that being said, here's what early fathers had to say about the Church being authoritative. Saint Irenaeus in about AD 200 wrote,

> As I have already observed, the Church, having received this preaching and this faith, although scattered throughout the whole world, yet, as if occupying but one house, carefully preserves it. She also believes these points [of doctrine] just as if she had but one soul, and one and the same heart, and she proclaims them, and teaches them,

---

[51] *The Fundamental Doctrines* 1:2 [AD 225]
[52] *Medicine Chest Against All Heresies* 61:6 [AD 375]

and hands them down, with perfect harmony, as if she possessed only one mouth.[53]

Here, Saint Irenaeus is saying that the Catholic Church proclaims the gospel directly from God Himself. He says we are possessed by one mouth. The clear implication here is that the mouth of God gives us teaching.

Here's another quote from Eusibius of Caesarea from the fourth century. He writes, "But the brightness of the Catholic Church proceeded to increase in greatness, for it ever held to the same points in the same way, and radiated forth to all the race of Greeks and barbarians the revenant, sincere, and free nature, and the sobriety and purity of the divine teaching as to conduct and thought."[54]

Eusibius is saying that the Catholic Church is great because it has held the same teachings. Given that this is true, it would stand to reason that the Church should be authoritative. After all, their teachings from Jesus and the apostles have not changed.

Here's another quote from Saint Augustine, perhaps the most famous of the early Church Fathers. He writes,

> The Catholic Church is the work of Divine Providence, achieved through the prophecies of the prophets, through the Incarnation and the teaching of Christ, through the journeys of the Apostles, through the suffering, the crosses, the blood and death of the martyrs, through the admirable lives of the Saints… When, then, we see so much help on God's part, so much progress and so much fruit, shall we hesitate to bury ourselves in the bosom of that Church? For starting from the Apostolic chair down through successions of bishops even unto the open confession of all mankind, it has possessed the Crown of teaching authority.[55]

---

[53] *Against Heresies* 2
[54] *Ecclesiastical History* 4, 7, 13
[55] *The Advantage of Believing* 35

Augustine says here that the Church is the work of divine nature (God) and that His word has been passed down through people throughout time. Since this Church had the authority to teach, he couldn't fathom why anyone would choose not to be Catholic.

So if we should be Catholic, what happens to those who are not? Here's what early Christians had to say.

Here's a quote from Saint Ignatius of Antioch. He writes,

> Be not deceived, my brethren: If anyone follows a maker of schism [i.e., is a schismatic], he does not inherit the kingdom of God; if anyone walks in strange doctrine [i.e., is a heretic], he has no part in the passion [of Christ]. Take care, then, to use one Eucharist, so that whatever you do, you do according to God: For there is one flesh of our Lord Jesus Christ, and one cup in the union of his blood; one altar, as there is one bishop, with the presbytery and my fellow servants, the deacons.[56]

Who would be a maker of schism but the man who started the reformation himself, Martin Luther? Moreover, wouldn't this mean that the heretical views of Protestants send them to Hell?

Here's another quote, slightly later, from Fulgentius of Ruspe, an early philosopher. He writes,

> Anyone who receives the Sacrament of Baptism, whether in the Catholic Church or in a heretical or schismatic one, receives the whole Sacrament; but salvation, which is the strength of the Sacrament, he will not have, if he has had the Sacrament outside the Catholic Church [and remains in deliberate schism]. He must therefore return to the Church, not so that he might receive again the Sacrament of Baptism, which

---

[56] *Letter to the Philadelphians* 3:3–4:1 [A.D. 110]

no one dare repeat in any baptized person, but so that he may receive eternal life in Catholic society, for the obtaining of which no one is suited who, even with the Sacrament of Baptism, remains estranged from the Catholic Church.[57]

Fulgentius is saying that it does not matter where the Sacrament of Baptism was performed, but salvation does not exist outside the Church.

Here's a quote from Lactantius, an early writer. In 307 he wrote,

It is, therefore, the Catholic Church alone which retains true worship. This is the fountain of truth; this, the domicile of faith; this, the temple of God. Whoever does not enter there or whoever does not go out from there, he is a stranger to the hope of life and salvation...Because, however, all the various groups of heretics are confident that they are the Christians and think that theirs is the Catholic Church, let it be known that this is the true Church, in which there is confession and penance and which takes a health-promoting care of the sins and wounds to which the weak flesh is subject.[58]

As Lactantius makes clear, the Catholic Church "retains true worship," and trying to be saved outside it is hearsay.

All things considered, the Catholic Church has a history of being the only apostolic, authoritative, and infallible Church in existence. Since this is the only Church that fits all these parameters, it would stand to reason that we should all be members of that religion. To deny this would be heretical and against the Word of God.

---

[57] *The Rule of Faith* 43 [A.D. 524]
[58] *Divine Institutes* 4:30:11–13 [A.D. 307]

Abuse, Indulgences, and the Crusades

I can't possibly write a book defending Catholicism without talking about the abuse, indulgences, and the crusades. Let's first start with the crusades. Let me set the scene. It's the early nine hundreds. Monasteries were leading revivals. The reformers there wanted to return to the basic principles of Catholicism. In doing this, they established new religious orders.

Influenced by religious devotion, popes began to reform the Church. They began to expand the Church's power. A new age of religious feeling was born—the Age of Faith. Still, many problems faced the Catholic Church. For example, some priests were illiterate for the most part and could barely read prayers. Along with this, many bishops cared more about their positions as feudal lords than about their duties as religious leaders.

Reformers of the Church were most concerned by three main issues. First, village priests were getting married and having families. These marriages were against the rulings of the Church even at the time. Next, bishops were selling positions in the Church, an act called simony. Simony can be divided into mental, conventional, and real. In mental simony, there is lacking anything outward. In conventional simony, an expressed or understood agreement is perceived. It is subdivided into merely conventional, when neither party has fulfilled any of the terms of the agreement, and mixed conventional, when one of the parties has at least partly complied with the assumed obligations. To the latter, subdivision may be referred to what has been aptly termed "confidential simony," in which a Church appointment is obtained for a certain person with the understanding that later, he will either resign in favor of the one through whom he obtained the position or divide with him the revenues. Simony is called real when the stipulations of the mutual agreement have been either partly or completely carried out by both parties. The Church has since disavowed these actions.[59]

Finally, kings appointed Church bishops. Kings did this because bishops controlled a lot of land and wealth. Both kings and popes wanted to appoint bishops who would support them and their policies.

Church reformers believed the Church alone should appoint bishops. Reform and church organization Pope Leo IX and Pope Gregory VII enforced church laws against simony and marriage of priests. The popes who followed Leo and Gregory reorganized the Church to continue the policy of reform. The pope's group of advisers was called the papal Curia. It developed canon law on matters such as Marriage, divorce, and inheritance. Diplomats for the pope traveled through Europe dealing with bishops and kings. In this way, the popes established their authority throughout Europe.

The Church also collected taxes. Contrary to popular belief, this money was not always used for immoral purposes. The Church used some of the money to perform services such as caring for those sick and poor. In fact, the Church operated most hospitals in medieval Europe.

The Age of Faith also inspired wars of conquest. In 1093, Alexius Comnenus, the Byzantine emperor, sent an appeal to Robert, Count of Flanders. The emperor asked for help against the Muslim Turks. They were threatening to conquer his capital. Pope Urban II also read that letter. Shortly after this appeal, he issued a call for a Crusade to gain control over the Holy Land. Over the next three hundred years, a number of such Crusades were launched. The Crusades had economic, social, and political goals as well as religious motives.

With red crosses sewn on over their armor and the battle cry of "God wills it!" knights and commoners were influenced by religion and became Crusaders.

---

[59] Catholic Answers (2019, February 22), Simony, Retrieved May 4, 2020.

All in all, the Crusaders had won a narrow strip of land. It stretched about 650 miles from Edessa in the north to Jerusalem in the south. The Second Crusade was organized to recapture the city of Jerusalem. But its armies went home in defeat.

In the 1200s, four more Crusades to free the Holy Land were also unsuccessful. The religious spirit of the First Crusade faded, and the search for personal gain grew. In two later Crusades, armies marched not to the Holy Land but to Egypt. The Crusaders intended to weaken Muslim forces there before going to the Holy Land. But none of these attempts had conquered many lands.

So, after that quick history lesson, here is something to consider. Catholics were attempting to conquer back the Holy Land. They were not slaughtering Muslims for no reason. While morally unacceptable, Catholics had reasons for what they were doing.

Another issue that has plagued the Church's history is the abuse and indulgences in the Church. Abuse of any kind is unacceptable and should not be tolerated in the Church whatsoever. Contrary to popular belief, the Church is not lenient with abusive priests.[60] Priests who are accused of assault are not allowed to practice priesthood while the trial is going on. Those proven innocent are allowed to go back to being priests. Those who are proven guilty are removed from the priesthood. The Church has, of course, covered up some abuse within. The most notable case would be Cardinal McCarrick. These cases are inexcusable, but to leave the Church because of bad people in the Church is crazy. It is also rather unfortunate that when a Lutheran pastor abuses someone, everyone views Him as immoral, and rightfully so. But no one claims that the Lutheran Church is immoral because of the actions of this pastor. Why can't we leave this same standard for the Catholic Church?

With all this being said, what are the actual numbers for priest abuse today? A study by Criminal Justice and Behavior estimates that about 4 percent of priests have been accused of sexual assault.[61] That's

---

[60] *Charter for the Protection of Children and Young People*

[61] Margaret Leland Smith, Andres F. Rengifo, and Brenda K. Vollman, "Trajectories of Abuse and Disclosure: Child Sexual Abuse by Catholic Priests," *Criminal Justice and Behavior* 35, no. 5 (2008): 570–582.

much too high, but it's on the low end of the average population for males. In Micheal Seto's Annual Review of Clinical Psychology, he said that 3 percent to 9 percent of male respondents acknowledge sexual fantasies or sexual contact involving prepubescent children.[62] Moreover, abuse is actually more prevalent in Protestant Churches than Catholic ones.[63] Contrary to popular belief, abuse is not a problem that is unique to the Catholic Church, or one that is more prevalent than in other societies.

Next, I'll discuss indulgences. The selling of indulgences was a massive reason for the Protestant reformation. However, the Church herself never taught that one's salvation could be sold. That is a myth promulgated by Protestant apologists. We had priests at the time going against the word of God much like Judas did during the time of Jesus. Would it be rational to leave Jesus because of Judas?

So, why did I bring up all these things in the same chapter? They seem rather different, do they not? No. The answer is that they don't matter. Yes, the Crusades, indulgences, and abuse all don't matter in today's world when discussing the true religion of God. Just because someone who has the same religious philosophy as you does something immoral does not mean that religious philosophy is wrong. Just because Catholics were selling indulgences in the 1500s or killing Muslims in the 1000s does not mean that Catholicism is not the true Word of God. If you still disagree, let me explain it a different way. If a republican president admitted to abusing women, Republicans would disavow him. However, they would not become Democrats. They would simply disavow the man who did the immoral thing. You would not leave Jesus because of Judas. Again, just because someone who is Catholic did something immoral does not mean that Catholicism is immoral. The Church does not teach murder and abuse to be moral.

---

[62] Michael C. Seto "Pedophilia." *Annual Review of Clinical Psychology* 5 (2009): 391–407.

[63] M. Blow (2019, May 30). "Is there more sexual abuse in the Protestant Churches than the Catholic Church?" Retrieved May 4, 2020.

The Sacrifice of the Mass

The Mass is one of the pinnacle parts of Catholic theology. Like everything else, it is not something that we have just made up. The Catholic Church did not one day declare that everyone needs to go to Mass without a biblical basis to back it up. Every single thing we do in the Mass has a basis in the Bible. The Sacrifice of the Mass is also unanimously attested to in the early church.

Trying to date the first Mass after the Last Supper would be rather difficult. It's quite possible that when the apostles heard "do this is in memory of me," they did it soon thereafter. We just have not infallibly declared it.

However, we do have letters from Early Church Fathers that talk about the Mass. Some are from the late first century.

Here's the earliest quote we have regarding the Mass from a nonbiblical source. It's from the Didache in AD 70. It writes,

> Assemble on the Lord's day, and break bread and offer the Eucharist; but first make confession of your faults, so that your sacrifice may be a pure one. Anyone who has a difference with his fellow is not to take part with you until he has been reconciled, so as to avoid any profanation of your sacrifice [Matt. 5:23–24]. For this is the offering of which the Lord has said, "Everywhere and always bring me a sacrifice that is undefiled, for I am a great king, says the Lord, and my name is the wonder of nations" [Mal. 1:11, 14].[64]

---

[64] *Didache* 14 [AD 70]

Here, we have the apostles telling people to assemble on the Lord's Day and receive Eucharist in a sacrificial manner. This is a clear allusion to the Catholic Mass. Here's another quote from one of the most famous Early Church Fathers, Saint Ignatius of Antioch. He writes,

> Make certain, therefore, that you all observe one common Eucharist; for there is but one Body of our Lord Jesus Christ, and but one cup of union with his Blood, and one single altar of sacrifice— even as there is also but one bishop, with his clergy and my own fellow servitors, the deacons. This will ensure that all your doings are in full accord with the will of God.[65]

Saint Ignatius of Antioch makes a reference to the sacrifice in which God gives us in the Mass. The next quote comes from Saint Justin Martyr:

> God speaks by the mouth of Malachi, one of the twelve [minor prophets], as I said before, about the sacrifices at that time presented by you: "I have no pleasure in you, says the Lord, and I will not accept your sacrifices at your hands; for from the rising of the sun to the going down of the same, my name has been glorified among the Gentiles, and in every place incense is offered to my name, and a pure offering, for my name is great among the Gentiles..." [Mal. 1:10–11]. He then speaks of those Gentiles, namely us [Christians] who in every place offer sacrifices to him, that is, the bread of the Eucharist and also the cup of the Eucharist.[66]

---

[65] *Letter to the Philadelphians* 4 [AD 110]
[66] *Dialogue with Trypho the Jew* 41 [AD 155]

He makes a clear reference to the sacrifice of the Mass. Needless to say, the sacrifice of the Mass is not something that Catholics just made up. The question still remains, however. How is the Mass a sacrifice? After all, if Jesus sacrificed Himself on the cross "once and for all," a sacrifice after that would be superfluous and unbiblical.

There are a couple of important things worth noting when talking about the Mass. First and foremost, we are not redoing the sacrifice of Jesus on Calvary. If we were, we would essentially be saying that that sacrifice is not enough and is necessary to redo. This nullifies the sacrifice on the cross. It is a different type of sacrifice— one without bloodshed. This is, of course, not to be confused with the blood of the covenant in the form of wine. The reason we call it a nonbloody sacrifice is because it is a sacrifice without killing. Jesus does not die to give us the Eucharist. Rather, He sacrifices Himself to God in the form of bread and wine. He is truly and really existent in the form of bread and wine. The physical appearance stays the same, but the reality changes.

But how can Jesus be present in the bread and wine when He is holding them? After all, He would essentially be holding Himself in His hands. This is difficult to understand for the human brain, make no mistake. Nevertheless, saying "God cannot do this" would undercut His omnipotence. Just because we do not understand His power does not mean that He cannot do something.

Be that as it may, every single thing that we do in the Mass is biblical from the beginning to the end. First things first, when we walk into church, we are greeted by greeters. Even this is biblical.[67] When we walk in, we genuflect in front of the altar and go into the pew. We do this in adoration to the most holy Sacrament of the altar. Since Catholics attest that the Eucharist is truly present in bread and wine, we admire it, and the altar on which the sacrifice is performed, with a genuflection.

The first thing we do in the Mass is sing while the priest and company process in. There are many verses in the Bible that talk about worship

---

[67] "100 Bible Verses about Greeting Others," Accessed July 28, 2020.

through song.[68] We start the Mass with the sign of the cross, a reference to the Trinity in Matthew 28:19. The priest then says "peace be with you." To which the congregation replies "and with your spirit." Giving peace to one another is also something that is referenced several times in the Bible.[69] We then are called to mind our sins and ask for forgiveness.[70] We acknowledge ourselves before we celebrate the mystery of the Eucharist.

The priest then calls to Jesus for mercy on us as sinners.[71] We give glory to God through singing or reciting the "Gloria." The first few words of the Gloria come from angels singing glory to God in Luke 2:14. We then listen to a reading from the Old Testament, a responsorial psalm (which is a prayer) and then another reading from a letter in the New Testament. After that, we listen to the Gospel and the priest's analysis of it. Next, we acknowledge our faith through the Apostle's Creed. Thereafter, we ask God for things through petitions.[72]

After this, not much happens that has not already been said other than the "Our Father." We sacrifice the lamb of God, consume Him, and depart after again making the sign of the cross.

All in all, the sacrifice of the Mass is biblical all of the way through. Despite what Protestants say, our traditions are not the traditions of men. Rather, they are the traditions of God. Because this service is biblical and historic, we should go. As I mentioned in the last chapter, the Catholic Church has the authority to tell you whether or not you should go to Mass. Since they have declared that it is a grave sin not to go to Mass, we need to go.

If you want to see more visual Eucharistic miracles, God gives us those as well.[73]

---

[68] "65 Bible Verses about Songs," What Does the Bible Say About Songs? Accessed July 28, 2020.

[69] "Bible Verses About Peace: 20 Great Scripture Quotes," What Christians Want to Know RSS. Accessed July 28, 2020.

[70] "100 Bible Verses about Asking for Forgiveness," What Does the Bible Say About Asking for Forgiveness? Accessed July 28, 2020.

[71] "89 Bible Verses about Asking for Mercy," Accessed July 28, 2020.

[72] "100 Bible Verses about Asking for Things," What Does the Bible Say About Asking for Things? Accessed July 28, 2020.

[73] Rychlak, Ronald. "Eucharistic Miracles: Evidence of the Real Presence." *Catholic Answers*, Catholic Answers, 23 July 2021.

Sacraments

Sacraments are an essential part to Catholic theology. They are sacred, hence the name. One cannot talk about Catholicism without discussing the Sacraments as well. Some say the Sacraments are not biblical, and the Church just made them up. Despite what Protestants may say, every Sacrament has a biblical and historical basis. In fact, no one denies any of the seven Sacraments in the early church. Some are more attested to than others, like Baptism (necessity and Baptism of infants) and Confession over Anointing of the Sick, but regardless, the point still stands.

The Sacrament that everyone receives first in the Catholic Church is the Sacrament of Baptism. Nearly every Christian believes that one must be baptized in order to have the ability to go to Heaven. As Jesus says in John 3:5, "Very truly I tell you, no one can enter the kingdom of God unless they are born of water and the Spirit."

As you can see, Jesus makes clear that one must be "born of water" in order to be able to enter the kingdom of God.

People who do not believe in "water Baptism" have said that this is referring to a natural birth. They seem to think it means "unless your mother's water breaks and you choose God afterward, you cannot enter the kingdom of God." However, this train of thought makes little sense when brought to its logical conclusion. If one cannot enter Heaven unless the woman's water is broken, what happens to babies who are aborted or miscarried? Do they go to Hell? People who don't believe in water Baptism don't believe in Purgatory, so if they are correct in saying that this verse is talking about a natural birth, and that Purgatory doesn't exist, then these babies have two options. They either go to Hell, or they cease to exist. Either way would be extremely hard to argue. As it stands, the notion that you must be physically born in order to have a chance at Heaven is extremely heretical and implies that God sends aborted babies to Hell through no fault of their own.

Here's another quote from the Gospel of Mark. In Mark 16:16, Jesus says, "Whoever believes and is baptized will be saved, but whoever does not believe will be condemned."

Jesus again makes clear that one must be baptized along with being a believer (which consists of following the commandments)[74] in order to be saved. Peter also commands that people be baptized in Acts 10:48.

As clearly shown, Jesus was adamant about people being baptized in order to go to Heaven. This belief is also shown by the early Church Fathers. Here's a quote from Justin Martyr in AD 151:

> Whoever are convinced and believe that what they are taught and told by us is the truth, and professes to be able to live accordingly, are instructed to pray and to beseech God in fasting for the remission of their former sins, while we pray and fast with them. Then they are led by us to a place where there is water, and they are reborn in the same kind of rebirth in which we ourselves were reborn: "In the name of God, the Lord and Father of all, and of our Savior Jesus Christ, and of the Holy Spirit," they receive the washing of water. For Christ said, "Unless you be reborn, you shall not enter the kingdom of Heaven."[75]

As shown here, we must be "reborn" with water in order to enter the kingdom of Heaven. He then reiterates this point by saying, "Unless you be reborn, you shall not enter the kingdom of Heaven."

[74.] Matthew 19:17

[75] *An international exhibition designed and created by Carlo acutis the servant of god.* MIRACOLI EUCARISTICI—Mostra Internazionale Ideata e Realizzata da Carlo Acutis e Nicola Gori. (n.d.). Retrieved July 29, 2022.

Here's another quote from Clement of Alexandria regarding the
necessity for Baptism in salvation:

> When we are baptized, we are enlightened. Being
> enlightened, we are adopted as sons. Adopted
> as sons, we are made perfect. Made perfect,
> we become immortal... "and sons of the Most
> High" [Ps. 82:6]. This work is variously called
> grace, illumination, perfection, and washing. It
> is a washing by which we are cleansed of sins, a
> gift of grace by which the punishments due our
> sins are remitted, an illumination by which we
> behold that holy light of salvation.[76]

As Clement of Alexandria clearly says, Baptism cleanses us of
our sins and that this is necessary for salvation.

However, the process of baptizing an adult would be different from that of baptizing an infant. So when the Bible talks about
preaching/believing then baptizing, in that order, it does not mean
that this is necessary for all those who receive Baptism. The scenarios in the Bible that talk about someone first believing then being
baptized always apply to adults. Catholics view Baptism in this way
for people who want to be baptized into the Church. If someone at
twenty wants to join the Church, we take them through RCIA and
make sure they believe before we baptize them.

Because Baptism is necessary for salvation, it would be beneficial
to baptize everyone. However, the manner in which we administer
Baptism for adults is divergent from the matter in which we baptize
infant children. Seeing that infants cannot cognitively make the decision for themselves regarding their theology of Catholicism, making a
decision for them that we can prove objectively through Bible verses
to be favorable for the child's soul would be beneficial. After all, if
someone dies without being baptized, Jesus makes clear what happens
to them. With that being said, there are exceptions. God is not bound

---

[76] *The Instructor of Children* 1:6:26:1 [AD 191]

by the Sacraments. A newborn who dies immediately after childbirth with no way of getting baptized may or may not go to Hell. I am not God; I am not the one to make those decisions. However, does this mean we should wait to baptize infants? Historical accounts from early Christians would suggest that we do not.

Here's a quote from Hippolytus regarding infant Baptism: "Baptize first the children, and if they can speak for themselves, let them do so. Otherwise, let their parents or other relatives speak for them." He wants the children to speak for themselves if they are able to. If not, parents should speak for them. We should not wait until individuals can make their own decision regarding Baptism.

Here's another quote from Gregory of Nazianzus, an early Church writer, in the year AD 399:

> Do you have an infant child? Allow sin no opportunity; rather, let the infant be sanctified from childhood. From his most tender age let him be consecrated by the Spirit. Do you fear the seal [of Baptism] because of the weakness of nature? Oh, what a pusillanimous mother and of how little faith!"[77]
>
> "Well enough," some will say, "for those who ask for Baptism, but what do you have to say about those who are still children, and aware neither of loss nor of grace? Shall we baptize them too?" Certainly [I respond], if there is any pressing danger. Better that they be sanctified unaware, than that they depart unsealed and uninitiated.[78]

Gregory of Nazianz clearly believes that we should baptize infants.

---

[77] *Oration on Holy Baptism* 40:7 [AD 388]
[78] Ibid., 40:28

Here's another quote from John Chrysostom regarding infant Baptism:

> You see how many are the benefits of Baptism, and some think its heavenly grace consists only in the remission of sins, but we have enumerated ten honors [it bestows]! For this reason we baptize even infants, though they are not defiled by [personal] sins, so that there may be given to them holiness, righteousness, adoption, inheritance, brotherhood with Christ, and that they may be his [Christ's] members.[79]

So if the early Church Fathers believed in infant Baptism, how early did the Church start doing it? As Origen clearly says,

> The Church received from the apostles the tradition of giving Baptism even to infants. The apostles, to whom were committed the secrets of the divine Sacraments, knew there are in everyone innate strains of [original] sin, which must be washed away through water and the Spirit."[80]
>
> "Every soul that is born into flesh is soiled by the filth of wickedness and sin… In the Church, Baptism is given for the remission of sins, and, according to the usage of the Church, Baptism is given even to infants. If there were nothing in infants which required the remission of sins and nothing in them pertinent to forgiveness, the grace of Baptism would seem superfluous.[81]

---

[79] *Baptismal Catecheses in Augustine, Against Julian* 1:6:21 [AD 388]
[80] *Commentaries on Romans* 5:9 [AD 248]
[81] *Homilies on Leviticus* 8:3 [AD 248]

As Origen makes clear, giving Baptism to infants is something that the Church has always done.

Lastly, in AD 252, the council of Carthage condemned the opinion that infants must wait until the eighth day after birth to be baptized.[82]

Baptism is required for salvation. Therefore, we need to baptize everyone, even those who do not fully understand it. In doing so, we raise the amount of people that are able to be saved.

However, the method of administering Baptism is debated. Some Baptist apologists will argue that because fully submerged Baptism is the only type of Baptism in the Bible, that is the only legitimate form of Baptism.

Except, both of these assumptions are false. The idea that Jesus and the eunuch were baptized fully submerged isn't definitive from a biblical standpoint. When it says they "came out of the water," it could be referring to them coming out of the river, after the Baptism. Moreover, even if it were true that they were baptized fully submerged, that does not necessarily mean that this is the only legitimate form of Baptism, much like the food Jesus eats in the Bible is not the only type of food that Christians are allowed to eat. Unless Jesus explicitly says we cannot eat a certain food, everything is fair game. This is the same with Baptism.

The next Sacrament that Catholics tend to receive next is the Sacrament of Reconciliation. Catholics receive the Sacrament of Reconciliation so that we may be forgiven of our sins.

> Therefore, if anyone is in Christ, the new creation has come: The old has gone, the new is here! All this is from God, who reconciled us to himself through Christ and gave us the ministry of Reconciliation: that God was reconciling the world to himself in Christ, not counting people's sins against them. And he has committed to us the message of Reconciliation. We are therefore

---

[82] St. Cyprian of Carthage, Letter 64 (59), 2

> Christ's ambassadors, as though God were mak-
> ing his appeal through us. We implore you on
> Christ's behalf: Be reconciled to God.[83]

As seen by this quote, Saint Paul says that God gave us the "ministry of Reconciliation" through Christ.

Some say this reconciliation is through Jesus alone and not a mediator, but it's important to remember that Jesus gave man authority to forgive sins in the Gospel of John: "If you forgive anyone's sins, their sins are forgiven; if you do not forgive them, they are not forgiven."[84] This very clearly states that if the apostles forgive sins, they are forgiven. As seen by the verse, Jesus gave the apostles the power and authority to forgive sins. A Protestant might ask, "Why does Jesus give us this Sacrament if we can go to him directly?" I am not fully aware as to why Jesus put this system in place. I do have some theories however. The first relates to the human nature of forgiveness. We have to have reassurance that we have done the right thing. We get that through confession. We do not get that reassurance through simply asking for forgiveness from God alone. It is also beneficial for a Church to know the sins of the congregation so that they may be addressed. A priest cannot call out a person directly, but he may do a homily on pornography if he is hearing a lot of confessions regarding that. Without telling your sins to the Church, he would have no idea. This theory makes sense when you look at James's commandment of sins to "one another" and not just God.[85] However, Protestants will argue that this verse does not prove the Catholic version of confession. Most will say that Jesus is not talking about confession, but the apostles' forgiveness against someone who has personally wronged them. This analysis of the verse doesn't make sense for a variety of reasons.

- Jesus tells the apostles that sins they forgive are forgiven, and sins they retain are retained. If Jesus meant sins (against

---

[83] 2 Corinthians 5:11–21
[84] John 20:23
[85] James 5:16

you), He would have said that. The implication here is that the apostles are able to forgive sins they had no part of. (As you will see soon, many ECFs viewed this verse the same way. In fact, it is unanimously attested to. Jesus, being God, would have known that people would view this verse in this way. Why not clear up any confusion simply by saying, "Against you"?)

- If Jesus actually meant for the apostles to only forgive sins that they were personally affected by, why even say it? After all, if Jesus said, "If you forgive someone in your heart, they are forgiven in your heart," the apostles wouldn't have thought twice about it. Why would Jesus even say this? We know this to be true even if Jesus doesn't say it explicitly because of human nature.
- Relating to the last point, if Jesus actually meant this the way the Protestants interpreted it, the apostles would have thought of it as common sense. If that were the case, why does John put it in his Gospel? Why put something of so little importance, when he also makes clear that not everything Jesus said was written down later in his Gospel?[86]
- This is said to the apostles only. It would seem to me that if Jesus were talking about forgiveness of personal transgression, He would have said this to a group of people other than the apostles.

Again, I'm not sure why exactly this system was set in place, but I am not one to go against God's clear command.

Confession is one of the things that we have the most writings on. All these letters are from early Christians who lived before there was a Bible. The first letter is from Ignatius of Antioch, a Catholic saint, in the year AD 110. He writes,

> For as many as are of God and of Jesus Christ are also with the bishop. And as many as shall,

---
[86.] John 21:25

in the exercise of penance, return into the unity of the Church, these, too, shall belong to God, that they may live according to Jesus Christ.[87] For where there is division and wrath, God does not dwell. To all them that repent, the Lord grants forgiveness, if they turn in penitence to the unity of God, and to communion with the bishop.[88]

Saint Ignatius is saying that we should repent to be in unity with God, and communion with the bishop. This would mean that the bishop is relevant and necessary in the process.

Another quote is by Tertullian, an early Christian philosopher. In 215 he wrote,

"[Some] people flee from [confession] as being an exposure of themselves, or they put it off from day to day. I presume they are more mindful of modesty than of salvation, like those who contract a disease in the more shameful parts of the body and shun making themselves known to the physicians; and thus they perish along with their own bashfulness... The Church has the power of forgiving sins. This I acknowledge and adjudge."[89]

He says that we should not only go to confession but we should not put it off either.

Yet another quote from another philosopher, Hippolytus in 215,

God and Father of our Lord Jesus Christ...pour forth now that power which comes from you, from your Royal Spirit, which you gave to your beloved Son, Jesus Christ, and which he bestowed upon his holy Apostles... And grant this your servant [the new bishop], whom you have chosen for the episcopate, [the power] to feed your holy

---

[87] *Letter to the Philadelphians* 3 [AD 110]
[88] *Letter to the Philadelphians* 3 [AD 106]
[89] *Repentance* 10:1 [AD 203]

flock and to serve without blame as your high priest, ministering night and day to propitiate unceasingly before your face and to offer to you the gifts of your holy Church, and by the Spirit of the high priesthood to have the authority to forgive sins, in accord with your command.[90]

Here, Hippolytus is saying that confession is an authority given to bishops through the apostles.

To further illustrate my point, John Chrysotom, Archbishop of Constantinople, in AD 387 wrote:

Priests have received a power which God has given neither to angels nor to archangels. It was said to them: "Whatsoever you shall bind on earth shall be bound in Heaven; and whatsoever you shall loose, shall be loosed." Temporal rulers have indeed the power of binding: but they can only bind the body. Priests, in contrast, can bind with a bond which pertains to the soul itself and transcends the very heavens. Did [God] not give them all the powers of Heaven? "Whose sins you shall forgive," He says, "they are forgiven them; whose sins you shall retain, they are retained." The Father has given all judgment to the Son. And now I see the Son placing all this power in the hands of men. They are raised to this dignity as if they were already gathered up to Heaven.[91]

Here, Chrysotom is referring to John 20:23. He explicitly states that this is referring to a literal forgiveness of sins, and that priests also have this power.

---

[90] *Apostolic Tradition* 3 [AD 215]
[91] *The Priesthood 3:5* [AD 387]

Here's another quote, slightly earlier, from Saint Hippolytus of Rome, a theologian in AD 215:

> God and Father of our Lord Jesus Christ… pour forth now that power which comes from you, from your Royal Spirit, which you gave to your beloved Son, Jesus Christ, and which He bestowed upon his holy Apostles… and grant this your servant [the new bishop], whom you have chosen for the episcopate, [the power] to feed your holy flock and to serve without blame as your high priest, ministering night and day to propitiate unceasingly before your face and to offer to you the gifts of your holy Church, and by the Spirit of the high priesthood to have the authority to forgive sins, in accord with your command.[92]

Both of these men explicitly state that priests have the authority to forgive sins. Saint Hippolytus is insisting that through the apostles, priests were given the authority to forgive sins, in accord with Jesus' command.

As these men reiterate, Jesus is talking about the objective forgiveness of sins in John 20:23, and not merely subjective forgiveness through a specific individual. Confession is also something that is necessary for the human heart. If I had a friend that I considered enormously valuable, and I did something that he or she didn't like, I would try to meet up in person to talk about it and ask for forgiveness. The human heart needs that reassurance in person to feel better. This is yet another reason why Jesus gives us the Sacrament of Reconciliation. He knows that the human heart needs that reassurance. Without it, you are just guessing as to whether or not God forgave you. Moreover, I alluded to earlier that only Catholic priests have the ability to forgive sins objectively through apostolic suc-

---

[92] *Apostolic Tradition* 3 [AD 215]

cession. In order to be sure our sins are forgiven, Jesus gives us the Sacrament of Reconciliation.

Generally, immediately after this, Catholic children receive the Sacrament of Communion. Eucharist is a practice by which most Protestants believe to be a representation of the Last Supper. But merely a representation at that. This does of course not line up with what the Bible says. We know that Exodus talks about how the Paschal Lamb had to be eaten:

"Then they shall eat the flesh on that night; roasted in fire, with unleavened bread *and* with bitter *herbs* they shall eat it[93]... In one house it shall be eaten; you shall not carry any of the flesh outside the house, nor shall you break one of its bones."[94]

Who is this lamb? It could be literal, but in the Gospel of John, Jesus is referred to as the "Lamb of God."[95] The book of Corinthians also talks about how Jesus was the Paschal Lamb that had to be sacrificed.[96]

We also know that Jesus truly turned the bread and wine into His body and blood.[97] However, the question still remains, on whether that power was given to others—namely, Catholic priests. Jesus insists that we all eat His flesh and drink His blood in the Gospel of John:

"Very truly I tell you, unless you eat the flesh of the Son of Man and drink his blood, you have no life in you. Whoever eats my flesh and drinks my blood has eternal life, and I will raise them up on the last day."[98]

Do we all have no life within us? Or did Jesus delegate power to administer His body and blood to others through him?

"It's just a symbol." It's a common argument by those who do not believe in transubstantiation. However, what did the early Church Fathers say about this?

---

[93] Exodus 12:8
[94] Exodus 12:46
[95] John 1:29
[96] 1 Corinthians 5:7
[97] Luke 22:19–20
[98] John 6:53

One would be Saint Ignatius of Antioch. In his letter to the Smyreans, he writes: "They hold aloof from the Eucharist and from services of prayer, because they refuse to admit that the Eucharist is the flesh of our Saviour Jesus Christ, which suffered for our sins and which, in his goodness, the Father raised."[99]

St. Ignatius is saying that the Eucharist is truly the body and blood of Christ.

Another would be the first defense of Saint Justin Martyr, written around AD 155. He says:

> And this food is called among us Εὐχαριστία [the Eucharist]... For not as common bread and common drink do we receive these; but in like manner as Jesus Christ our Savior, having been made flesh by the Word of God, had both flesh and blood for our salvation, so likewise have we been taught that the food which is blessed by the prayer of His word ["this is my Body"], and from which our blood and flesh by transmutation are nourished, is the flesh and blood of that Jesus who was made flesh. For the Apostles, in the memoirs composed by them, which are called Gospels, have thus delivered unto us what was enjoined upon them; that Jesus took bread, and when He had given thanks, said, "This do in remembrance of Me, [Luke 22:19] this is My body"; and that, after the same manner, having taken the cup and given thanks, He said, "This is My blood"; and gave it to them alone.[100]

St. Justin Martyr is insisting that when Jesus says "this is my body" and "this is my blood," he means it to be literal. He specifically refers to the Gospels and reiterates that Jesus is being literal when He

---

[99] *Letter to the Smyrnaeans* 6:2–7:1 [AD 110]
[100] *First Apology* 66 [AD 151]

says "this is my body" and "this is my blood." We must not only partake in the Eucharist, but you must be Catholic in order to receive.

Here's another quote from another philosopher. Tertullian, in 210, wrote,

> [T]here is not a soul that can at all procure salvation, except it believe whilst it is in the flesh, so true is it that the flesh is the very condition on which salvation hinges. And since the soul is, in consequence of its salvation, chosen to the service of God, it is the flesh which actually renders it capable of such service. The flesh, indeed, is washed [in Baptism], in order that the soul may be cleansed... the flesh is shadowed with the imposition of hands [in Confirmation], that the soul also may be illuminated by the Spirit; the flesh feeds [in the Eucharist] on the body and blood of Christ, that the soul likewise may be filled with God.[101]

As Tertullian is insisting here, we *must* receive communion in order to be saved. "[T]he flesh is the very condition on which salvation hinges." Tertullian believed that receiving communion was not only righteous for salvation, but a necessity.

Another quote from Hippolytus:

> "And she [Wisdom] has furnished her table" [Prov. 9:2]... refers to his [Christ's] honored and undefiled body and blood, which day by day are administered and offered sacrificially at the spiritual divine table, as a memorial of that first and ever-memorable table of the spiritual divine supper [i.e., the Last Supper].[102]

---

[101] *The Resurrection of the Dead* 8 [AD 210]
[102] [i.e., the Last Supper]" (Fragment from *Commentary on Proverbs* [AD 217])

Hippolytus is saying that Proverbs 9:2 is in fact referring to the Holy Eucharist. Which is administered day by day and offered sacrificially at the table (altar). Notice how he says "body and blood" and not "bread and wine." This shows that Hippolytus, an early Church philosopher, believed in transubstantiation.

So if these early philosophers believed that it was truly body and blood, shouldn't we all? Some may say, "Look at it! It looks the same, so how could it be body and blood? It looks like bread!" When Jesus turned bread and wine into body and blood at the Last Supper, did the bread turn into Jesus's foot? Or did the reality change with the look remaining the same? With the wine, did it turn into and taste like Jesus's blood? No, of course not. It looked like wine, tasted like wine, but the reality is different from what is observed.

So if it is truly body and blood, are Catholics cannibals for receiving the Eucharist? Simply put, no. Receiving the Eucharist of Jesus Christ is not the same as cannibalism. Tom Nash from Catholic Answers puts it greatly:

"Cannibalism, simply put, is the eating of human flesh, typically after a person has died. A corpse (dead body) is usually present, or at least a dead body part. Second, the quantity of the flesh diminishes as it is being consumed. Third, digesting flesh results in physical nourishment, protein included."[103]

In Eucharist, we are receiving not the dead body of Christ, but the living sacrifice in Heaven. His body is not becoming withered away because of the Eucharist.

It would stand to reason that Jesus changed the reality to body and blood at the Last Supper. Moreover, if it's truly body and blood, then we should show respect to the Eucharist and the altar on which the Sacrament is performed. Catholics do this by bowing to the altar and to the Eucharistic presence of Jesus.

In order to become a full-fledged member of the Catholic Church, one must be confirmed in the Church. The word "Confirmation" is not mentioned in the Bible, but several groups were "sealed with the

---

[103] T. Nash (2019, August 5), Is Receiving the Eucharist Cannibalism? Retrieved June 12, 2020.

promised Holy Spirit" which is what Confirmation is. Here are a few Bible verses that talk about being sealed with the Holy Spirit:

"Then Paul placed his hands on them, the Holy Spirit came on them, and they spoke in tongues and prophesied."[104]

For those unfamiliar, this is exactly what Confirmation is for Catholics. The bishop (or whomever he authorizes) places his hands on those getting confirmed. In fact, we have instructions on this in the book of Hebrews.[105]

St. Paul also imposed his hands on those who were baptized, and they received the Holy Spirit.

"When the Apostles in Jerusalem heard that Samaria had accepted the Word of God, they sent Peter and John to Samaria. When they arrived, they prayed for the new believers there that they might receive the Holy Spirit, because the Holy Spirit had not yet come on any of them; they had simply been baptized in the name of the Lord Jesus. Then Peter and John placed their hands on them, and they received the Holy Spirit."[106]

Very clearly, this quote is saying that we need to receive the Holy Spirit through the laying of the hands, and not merely be baptized.

Despite not having many Bible verses, Confirmation (or the laying of the hands) is something that we have several historical accounts of.

Here's a quote from Hippolytus in AD 215:

> The bishop, imposing his hand on them, shall make an invocation, saying, "O Lord God, who made them worthy of the remission of sins through the Holy Spirit's washing unto rebirth, send into them your grace so that they may serve you according to your will, for there is glory to you, to the Father and the Son with the Holy Spirit, in the holy Church, both now and through the ages

---

[104] Acts 19:6
[105] Hebrews 6:2
[106] Acts 8:14–17

of ages. Amen." Then, pouring the consecrated oil into his hand and imposing it on the head of the baptized, he shall say, "I anoint you with holy oil in the Lord, the Father Almighty, and Christ Jesus and the Holy Spirit." Signing them on the forehead, he shall kiss them and say, "The Lord be with you." He that has been signed shall say, "And with your spirit." Thus shall he do to each.[107]

This quote again shows that the Sacrament of Confirmation's necessity and practice has not changed.

Lastly, here's a quote from an early Church Father named Pacian of Barcelona, who says that Baptism and Confirmation are both vitally important:

"If, then, the power of both Baptism and Confirmation, greater by far than charisms, is passed on to the bishops, so too is the right of binding and loosing."[108]

As you can see, the Bible mentions it, and many early Church Fathers believed in a laying of the hands, or what Catholics call Confirmation.

After this, Catholics usually get married. It's a sacred thing in the Church. Saint Paul even gives us rules for Marriage in the book of Ephesians:

> Submit to one another out of reverence for Christ. Wives, submit yourselves to your own husbands as you do to the Lord. For the husband is the head of the wife as Christ is the head of the Church, his body, of which he is the Savior. Now as the Church submits to Christ, so also wives should submit to their husbands in everything. Husbands, love your wives, just as Christ loved the Church and gave himself up for her to make

---

[107] *The Apostolic Tradition* 21–22 [AD 215]
[108] *Three Letters to the Novatianist Sympronian* 1:6 [AD 383]

her holy, cleansing her by the washing with water through the word, and to present her to himself as a radiant Church, without stain or wrinkle or any other blemish, but holy and blameless. In this same way, husbands ought to love their wives as their own bodies. He who loves his wife loves himself. After all, no one ever hated their own body, but they feed and care for their body, just as Christ does the Church—for we are members of his body. For this reason a man will leave his father and mother and be united to his wife, and the two will become one flesh. This is a profound mystery—but I am talking about Christ and the Church. However, each one of you also must love his wife as he loves himself, and the wife must respect her husband.[109]

As seen by the text, Saint Paul wants the husband and wife to love each other as God has loved the Church. Jesus also says in Matthew's gospel that Marriage is something joined together by God:

"Therefore a man shall leave his father and his mother and hold fast to his wife, and the two shall become one flesh? So they are no longer two but one flesh. What therefore God has joined together, let not man separate."[110]

In the book of Hebrews, the writer also says that marriage should be "honored":

"Marriage should be honored by all, and the marriage bed kept pure, for God will judge the adulterer and all the sexually immoral."[111]

Since marriage is sacred, it should be considered a one-time thing. After all, if one can just get out of marriage at any time, there is not much sacred about it. We have several Bible verses of Jesus

---

[109] Ephesians 5:21–33
[110] Matthew 19:5–6
[111] Hebrews 13:4

condemning divorce and remarriage. As Jesus says in the Gospel of Matthew,

> But I tell you that anyone who divorces his wife, except for sexual immorality, makes her the victim of adultery, and anyone who marries a divorced woman commits adultery. Again, you have heard that it was said to the people long ago, "Do not break your oath, but fulfill to the Lord the vows you have made."[112]

Jesus refers to Marriage and divorce in this passage then says "do not break your oath," referring to divorce. Later in that same Gospel, he reiterates this statement: "At the beginning the Creator made them male and female, and said, 'For this reason a man will leave his father and mother and be united to his wife, and the two will become one flesh. So they are no longer two, but one flesh.' Therefore what God has joined together, let no one separate."[113]

God is saying that Marriage is bound together by God and should not be separated. The philosophy that divorce and remarriage is sinful is reiterated a couple of other times throughout the Bible.[114] Marriage is something that is sacred, and should be protected at all costs. Divorce is something that Jesus violently taught against. However with that being said, there are a few exceptions to this rule:

1. At least one partner didn't fully and freely consent.
2. Someone wasn't mature enough to understand the full extent of what they were doing.
3. There was never intent to be faithful.
4. One or both partners did not intend to be open to children.

---

[112] Matthew 5:32–33
[113] Matthew 19:4–6
[114] Mark 10:11–12; Luke 16:18

These rules are rather ambiguous; it's the reason annulments in the Church take so long. They do not want divorce to be something that anyone can do. Once again, this is done because the Sacrament of Matrimony is sacred, and we want to keep it that way.

The early Christians also agreed that divorce and remarriage is not adultery. Here's a quote from Hermas in AD 80:

"What then shall the husband do, if the wife continue in this disposition [adultery]? Let him divorce her, and let the husband remain single. But if he divorce his wife and marry another, he too commits adultery."[115]

Very clearly, Hermas believed that divorce and remarriage is sinful. Clement of Alexandria says something similar about seventy-five years later:

> That Scripture counsels Marriage, however, and never allows any release from the union, is expressly contained in the law: "You shall not divorce a wife, except for reason of immorality." And it regards as adultery the marriage of a spouse, while the one from whom a separation was made is still alive. "Whoever takes a divorced woman as wife commits adultery," it says; for "if anyone divorce his wife, he debauches her"; that is, he compels her to commit adultery. And not only does he that divorces her become the cause of this, but also he that takes the woman and gives her the opportunity of sinning; for if he did not take her, she would return to her husband.[116]

Clement of Alexandria denounces divorce along with marrying people who are divorced. About forty years later, Origen says something similar: "Just as a woman is an adulteress, even though she seem to be married to a man, while a former husband yet lives,

---

[115] *The Shepherd* 4:1:6 [AD 80]
[116] *Miscellanies* 2:23:145:3 [AD 208]

so also the man who seems to marry her who has been divorced does not marry her, but, according to the declaration of our Savior, he commits adultery with her."[117]

Origen believes that you cannot remarry if your former husband is alive. This would mean that divorce and remarriage is not acceptable.

The reason for marriage is rather explicit in the Bible. In the book of Genesis, Moses says to "be fruitful and multiply."[118] As I'll show through early Church Father quotes, they also believed that sexual acts without the openness to have children is sinful. Here's another quote from Clement of Alexandria on immorality of sexual acts outside marriage: "Because of its divine institution for the propagation of man, the seed is not to be vainly ejaculated, nor is it to be damaged, nor is it to be wasted."[119] He then makes clear what he means in the later quote: "To have coitus other than to procreate children is to do injury to nature."[120]

As Clement of Alexandria makes clear that sexual acts (those that involve intended ejaculation) are sinful unless there is intent to be open to children.

Lactantius makes clear that sex is not supposed to be for "pleasure." Rather, its intent is for the "needs of life." To conclude, he says that [sex] is "received by us for no other purpose than the generation of offspring."

Before I move on to the next Sacrament, it's vitally important that I stress that the Bible and earliest Christians both agreed that homosexual marriages and acts were against the Word of God. Contrary to popular belief, this is not a homophobic thing. Being attracted to the same sex is not actually considered a sin in the Church. However, the purpose of marriage is to produce children. Biologically, homosexual marriages cannot bear children. Therefore, homosexual people should not get married. If they don't get married, it is sinful to have sexual relations with anyone. That is why Saint Paul says that active

---

[117] *Commentaries on Matthew* 14:24 [AD 248]
[118] Genesis 1:27–28 (Genesis 9:1; 35:11)
[119] *The Instructor of Children* 2:10:91:2 [AD 191]
[120] Ibid., 2:10:95:3

homosexuals will not inherit the kingdom of God.[121] Keep in mind, "active" homosexuals would mean that someone is actively doing homosexual acts, not merely those who are attracted to the same sex.

The argument then becomes "Why would God make people gay if it's a sin to have intercourse with a member of the same sex?" The answer is, the same reason unmarried men are sexually attracted to women they are not married to even though it would be sinful to do so. We all have temptations we must overcome.

Someone may have the vocation to do pastoral work and not be married. In order to do this in the Church, one would have to go through the Sacrament of Holy Orders. This Sacrament, like the others, was unanimously accepted in the early church. The three-fold ministry is not something that is explicit in Scripture, but unanimous in the early church

This process has been the same for centuries. In the book of Titus, Saint Paul instructs him to appoint presbyters in every town.[122] Some will argue that Peter calls everyone priests, which he technically does.[123] However, this only means it in a very specific sense. This is known as the "priesthood of the faithful" and applies to all believers. However, ministerial priesthood is completely different, even from a biblical perspective. As Luke writes in the book of Acts, you have certain "overseers" in a Church.

"Keep watch over yourselves and all the flock of which the Holy Spirit has made you overseers. Be shepherds of the Church of God, which he bought with his own blood."[124]

As you can see, there should be a certain hierarchy in the Church. The process of administering this hierarchy is clear in the book of Acts. First, Luke describes the laying of the hands.[125] In his first letter to Timothy, Saint Paul references this action: "Do not neglect your gift, which was given you through prophecy when the

---

[121] 1 Corinthians 6:9
[122] Titus 1:5
[123] 1 Peter 2:9
[124] Acts 20:28
[125] Acts 6:6, 13:3

body of elders laid their hands on you."[126] Saint Paul is referring to a certain group of people that have a gift that was given to them "when the body of elders laid their hands." It would be rational to assume that Saint Paul is referencing priesthood and Sacraments here. The "gift" could mean the gift of preaching, or something along those lines. However, an elder in your Church laying his hands on someone does not help them teach the Word of God. Therefore, it's rather judicious to assume that it's something more special than just teaching the Word of God or being a leader in the Church.

In Saint Paul's second letter to Timothy, he says a similar thing: "For this reason I remind you to fan into flame the gift of God, which is in you through the laying on of my hands."[127] As Saint Paul and Luke make apparent, the "laying of the hands" is sacred and gives the person receiving it a special gift. However, should this gift be given to everyone who wants it, or merely specific people? In the Catholic Church, we only allow males to be priests. This is largely due to the fact that God came to Earth as a man, and all of His apostles were men. Therefore, the first Catholic bishops were all men. The Church does not feel as if they have the authority to change this. This does not diminish the role of women in the Church. The Church is like filming a movie. Each role is of vital importance, and without even one, the entire project comes tumbling down. The role that women play in the Church is not less salient; rather, merely divergent.

If we only allow men to be pastors, an appropriate name for them would be to call them *father*. After all, they do "father" the Church and look after her. Someone may say, "But doesn't the Bible say 'Call no man *father*'?"[128] There are several instances of people being called "father" in the Bible. It would stand to reason, therefore, that it's okay to call men "father."

For example, here's an excerpt from the book of Acts: "To this he replied: 'Brothers and fathers, listen to me! The God of glory

---

[126] 1 Timothy 4:14
[127] 2 Timothy 1:6
[128] Matthew 23:9

appeared to our father Abraham while he was still in Mesopotamia, before he lived in Harran.'"[129]

The book of Hebrews talks about how there are earthly fathers to discipline us:

> Endure hardship as discipline; God is treating you as his children. For what children are not disciplined by their father? If you are not disciplined—and everyone undergoes discipline—then you are not legitimate, not true sons and daughters at all. Moreover, we have all had human fathers who disciplined us and we respected them for it. How much more should we submit to the Father of spirits and live!

As you can see, the author of this verse calls another man "father."

In his letter to the Romans, Saint Paul also calls Abraham the "father to us all":

> Therefore, the promise comes by faith, so that it may be by grace and may be guaranteed to all Abraham's offspring—not only to those who are of the law but also to those who have the faith of Abraham. He is the father of us all. As it is written: "I have made you a father of many nations." He is our father in the sight of God, in whom he believed—the God who gives life to the dead and calls into being things that were not.[130]

As you can see, Saint Paul calls Abraham "father" a couple of times in these verses.

---

[129] Acts 7:2
[130] Romans 4:16–17

First Thessalonians also talks about how a group of people treat someone as a father treats his children: "For you know that we dealt with each of you as a father deals with his own children."[131]

Saint Paul also tells the Corinthians that he became their father through the Gospel: "I am writing this not to shame you but to warn you as my dear children. Even if you had ten thousand guardians in Christ, you do not have many fathers, for in Christ Jesus I became your father through the Gospel."[132]

Finally, in the first book of John, he calls a group of people "fathers":

> I am writing to you, fathers, because you know Him who is from the beginning. I am writing to you, young men, because you have overcome the evil one. I write to you, children, because you know the Father. I write to you, fathers, because you know him who is from the beginning. I write to you, young men, because you are strong, and the word of God abides in you, and you have overcome the evil one.[133]

Clearly, John is referencing a group of people as "fathers."

If it's not okay to call people "fathers," why did so many apostles do it? Clearly, it's acceptable to call people "father," as seen from these Bible verses. So what is Jesus saying when he says to call no man "father"? Obviously, this means we should call no one our God except the Father. This is not saying call no one "father." It says "call no one *your* father." Meaning, calling someone Father (name) is perfectly acceptable from a biblical standpoint.

Priests are also asked to be celibate. Many Protestants disagree with this. Why can't a pastor love his wife and his Church? Why do priests have to remain celibate? Well, there are a few answers to this.

---

[131] 1 Thessalonians 2:11
[132] 1 Corinthians 4:14–17
[133] 1 John 2:13–15

Firstly, Christ was celibate. This is done in reference to Him. Some may say that forbidding Marriage is a doctrine of demons[134] and that a bishop may be married once.[135] However, there are a couple of things worth noting. Number one, technically we could have a priest that is married. It isn't an outright restriction. Although generally, priests take a vow of celibacy. Secondly, the context is clearly talking about the end times. Priests in the Latin rite have not been able to marry for almost 1000 years. Have the end times been happening for 1000 years? That being said, the Church still believes that Marriage is a holy symbol of Christ. In the book of Ephesians, Saint Paul talks about how wives and husbands must love each other:

> Submit to one another out of reverence for Christ. Wives, submit yourselves to your own husbands as you do to the Lord. For the husband is the head of the wife as Christ is the head of the Church, his body, of which he is the Savior. Now as the Church submits to Christ, so also wives should submit to their husbands in everything. Husbands, love your wives, just as Christ loved the Church and gave himself up for her to make her holy, cleansing her by the washing with water through the word, and to present her to himself as a radiant Church, without stain or wrinkle or any other blemish, but holy and blameless. In this same way, husbands ought to love their wives as their own bodies. He who loves his wife loves himself. After all, no one ever hated their own body, but they feed and care for their body, just as Christ does the Church—for we are members of his body. For this reason a man will leave his father and mother and be united to his wife, and the two will become one flesh. This is a profound

---

[134] 1 Timothy 4:3
[135] 1 Timothy 3:2

mystery—but I am talking about Christ and the Church. However, each one of you also must love his wife as he loves himself, and the wife must respect her husband.

As seen by the text, Saint Paul wants the husband and wife to love each other as God has loved the Church. It's also recommended by Saint Paul in his letter to the Corinthians that ministers remain celibate.

I would like you to be free from concern. An unmarried man is concerned about the Lord's affairs—how he can please the Lord. But a married man is concerned about the affairs of this world—how he can please his wife—and his interests are divided. An unmarried woman or virgin is concerned about the Lord's affairs: Her aim is to be devoted to the Lord in both body and spirit. But a married woman is concerned about the affairs of this world—how she can please her husband. I am saying this for your own good, not to restrict you, but that you may live in a right way in undivided devotion to the Lord.

Saint Paul clearly believes that pastors should remain unmarried so that they may devote all their lives to the Church. But why is this? Why would a priest be better off unmarried and celibate? Can't he love a wife and the Church? The answer is yes, but it could cause some problems. For one, if a priest's wife is going into labor and someone wants Anointing of the Sick (one of the seven Sacraments), whom does he choose? If unmarried and celibate, he does not have to make that decision. Making sure priests remain celibate and unmarried helps them put all their life and effort into the Church.

Last but certainly not least, we have the Sacrament of Anointing of the Sick. There are only a couple of Bible verses referencing this

Sacrament. The fist would be in the Gospel of Mark when the apostles are anointing people with oil and curing them of their illnesses:

"They went out and preached that people should repent. They drove out many demons and anointed many sick people with oil and healed them."[136] The apostles, through the power of Christ, are healing people. This is what Anointing of the Sick is.

The other verse is in the book of James when he tells, "Is anyone among you sick? Let them call the elders of the Church to pray over them and anoint them with oil in the name of the Lord. And the prayer offered in faith will make the sick person well; the Lord will raise them up. If they have sinned, they will be forgiven."[137]

This is exactly what Anointing of the Sick is. Although there are only a couple of verses in the Bible that reference this Sacrament, those verses are abundantly clear, and their allusion is evident.

Like every other Sacrament, there are several quotes from early Church Fathers regarding Anointing of the Sick. The first would be a quote from John Chrysostom. Referencing the priesthood, he says,

> The priests of Judaism had power to cleanse the body from leprosy—or rather, not to cleanse it at all, but to declare a person as having been cleansed… Our priests have received the power not of treating with the leprosy of the body, but with spiritual uncleanness; not of declaring cleansed, but of actually cleansing… Priests accomplish this not only by teaching and admonishing, but also by the help of prayer. Not only at the time of our regeneration [in Baptism], but even afterward, they have the authority to forgive sins: "Is there anyone among you sick? Let him call in the priests of the Church, and let them pray over him, anointing him with oil in the name of the Lord. And the prayer of faith

---

[136] Mark 6:12–13
[137] James 5:14–15

shall save the sick man, and the Lord shall raise him up, and if he has committed sins, he shall be forgiven."[138]

Chrysostom is making an allusion to priests not only in their ability to forgive sin but also their ability to heal the sick.

The next quote is from Caesar of Arles, writing about a healing oil:

> As often as some infirmity overtakes a man, let him who is ill receive the body and blood of Christ; let him humbly and in faith ask the presbyters for blessed oil, to anoint his body, so that what was written may be fulfilled in him: "Is anyone among you sick? Let him bring in the presbyters, and let them pray over him, anointing him with oil; and the prayer of faith will save the sick man, and the Lord will raise him up; and if he be in sins, they will be forgiven him... See to it, brethren, that whoever is ill hasten to the Church, both that he may receive health of body and will merit to obtain the forgiveness of his sins."[139]

Caesar writes about oil and a prayer that will save a sick man. Again, this is what the Sacrament consists of.

The last quote is from Bishop Serapion in *The Sacramentary of Serapion*:

> We beseech you, Savior of all men, you that have all virtue and power, Father of our Lord and Savior Jesus Christ, and we pray that you send down from Heaven the healing power of the only-be-

---

[138] *On the Priesthood* 3:6:190ff [AD 387]
[139] *Sermons* 13[325]:3 [AD 542]

gotten [Son] upon this oil, so that for those who are anointed… it may be effected for the casting out of every disease and every bodily infirmity… for good grace and remission of sins.[140]

Bishop Serapion wants Jesus to send down the healing power of Jesus upon this oil so that diseases may be cast out. Moreover, this is another clear reference to the Sacrament of Anointing of the Sick.

Overall, despite what Protestants say, there are clear biblical and historical sources for every Sacrament. Catholics did not just make them up. That being said, we should strive to participate in these Sacraments since they give us the grace of God in a unique way.

---

[140] *The Sacramentary of Serapion* 29:1 [AD 350]

Mary

The philosophy of saints is imperative to Catholic theology. The communion of saints is something that every Catholic needs to associate with and strive to be inherent to. This chapter will defend the Catholic theologies regarding saints but will focus on the most important one primarily—Mary, the mother of our Lord. In this chapter I defend 3 of the 4 Marian dogmas—the mother of God, the perpetual virginity, and the sinlessness of Mary. (If I tried to defend all of the Church's dogmas, this book would be several thousand pages long). The two former are unanimously attested to in the early church, whereas the latter is not.

Because this book defends Catholic theology, it's imperative that I talk about Mary. Mary is vitally important in Catholic philosophy. Unfortunately, Protestants do not praise her as she deserves. Some Protestant theologians even believe that Mary was just the mortal mother of Jesus and not the mother of God. However, even from a nonbiblical perspective, this philosophy makes zero sense. If Jesus is God, and Mary is the mother of Jesus, then Mary is the mother of God. But what does the Bible say about this? In the Gospel of Matthew, an angel appears in a dream to Joseph and tells him, "The virgin [Mary] will conceive and give birth to a son, and they will call him Immanuel" (which means "God with us").[141] And in the Gospel of Luke, Elizabeth refers to Mary as the "mother of my Lord."[142] To deny that Mary is the mother of God would be the same thing as denying that Jesus is God.

---

[141] Matthew 1:23
[142] Luke 1:43

With Mary, Catholics pray to her in the Hail Mary. Most Protestants will hear the title of this prayer and immediately think it goes against what the Bible says, as we should worship no one but God. However, as I will reiterate further, Catholics do not worship Mary. Rather, they praise her as being sinless and a great role model. Praise and worship do not mean the same thing.

For reference, here is an example. Imagine your friend just got a really high grade on a math test that he studied really hard for. You would praise him by saying, "You're awesome! Good job!" This is clearly not a worshipping gesture. You would not worship someone for doing something like that. Catholics do not worship Mary; we praise her.

The Hail Mary, for those who do not know, takes its lines from biblical passages. "Hail Mary, full of grace, the Lord is with you,[143] blessed are you among women, and blessed is the fruit of your womb Jesus.[144] Holy Mary, Mother of God,[145] pray for us sinners,[146] now, and at the hour of our death, Amen." Despite what Protestants will say, the Hail Mary is biblical.

One of the main arguments regarding Mary is whether or not she was sinless. Protestants will cite Bible verses that say "all have sinned"[147] and Mary when she calls God her "savior"[148] (implying that if Mary needed a savior, she would have sinned).

However, neither of these points hold any value in debate. Firstly, when even Catholics say "everyone sins," this is a general rule. It does not negate exceptions. Jesus was fully man but did not sin. But then the argument against it would be, "Yes; however, Jesus was God. Therefore, He does not count." Actually, He would. Because if you read that verse and say, "That means every man sins; no dispensations." You have to then argue that Jesus was not fully God and fully man, or that Jesus was a sinner. If one of these is true, then

[143] Luke 1:28
[144] Luke 1:42
[145] Luke 1:43
[146] James 5:16
[147] Romans 3:23
[148] Luke 1:47

the Christian faith is erroneous down to the core teaching that God became man. If Saint Paul was actually referring to everyone without exceptions, Jesus would have been sinful, or not fully man.

Saint Paul is also only talking about personal sin. If I say that I have sinned, I am talking about something I did that was sinful. One would not hold a newborn baby and say "he has sinned." Rather, the saying would be, "He has sin on his soul. Let us clean it through Baptism." Babies that die right after birth cannot sin. So, obviously, there are certain exceptions to this "all have sinned" rule. If there are exceptions to the "all have sinned" quote from Saint Paul, then why reject Mary from this presumption?

"There are exceptions but Mary is not one of them. She needed a savior. She says so in the Gospel of Luke," my Protestant friends will say. This is a good argument in the sense that we all believe we need a savior because we are sinful and we need to be saved. Following this same logic flow, it would stand to reason that Mary needed a savior because she sinned.

It's imperative to point out that the Catholic Church does not scribble this verse out of her Bibles. We agree with the Protestants that Mary needed a savior—just in a unique way. She needed a savior, but not for the same reason that we need one. If Mary was sinless, this means she was "saved" from sin, and that Jesus was her savior. Simply put, you cannot make the argument that Mary was sinful with either of those Bible verses.

This argument is difficult to have from a merely biblical perspective. The Bible says that all have sinned. However, does this include Mary? It never says that Mary was sinless in the Bible. However, why would Jesus be in the womb of a sinner? He would have had to have grown and developed inside a woman with sin. With that being said, these are merely hypotheticals. Keep in mind that even if Mary was sinless, this does not dismantle the idea of a free will. If Mary was sinless, she could have just not had the desire to sin. Much like when some of us get to Heaven, we will no longer have the desire to sin.

Here are a few early Church Father quotes regarding Mary's sinless nature. Here's one from Ephraim the Syrian, an early philosopher, in AD 361. He writes,

"You alone and your Mother are more beautiful than any others, for there is no blemish in you nor any stains upon your Mother. Who of my children can compare in beauty to these?"[149]

"There are no stains upon your mother." It can be inferred here that they are talking about sin. There are no stains upon my mother, therefore there are no sins.

Augustine, a pristine Catholic theologian, had this to say about Mary's sinlessness:

> Having excepted the holy Virgin Mary, concerning whom, on account of the honor of the Lord, I wish to have absolutely no question when treating of sins—for how do we know what abundance of grace for the total overcoming of sin was conferred upon her, who merited to conceive and bear him in whom there was no sin?—so, I say, with the exception of the Virgin, if we could have gathered together all those holy men and women, when they were living here, and had asked them whether they were without sin, what do we suppose would have been their answer?[150]

Augustine makes clear that Mary is the exception for the "everyone sins" rule.

Here's another quote from John the Theologian. As his name suggests, he was an early philosopher for the Catholic Church. In AD 400, he wrote, "And from that time forth all knew that the spotless and precious body had been transferred to paradise."[151] Here, John the Theologian is talking about Mary's spotless body. What else could he be referring to other than sin? There is no other scenario.

So if Mary did not sin, she wouldn't have died. In Romans 6:23, Saint Paul says that the punishment for sin is death. If Mary never

---

[149] *The Passing of the Virgin* 16:2–17 [AD 300]
[150] *Nature and Grace* 36:42 [AD 415]
[151] *The Falling Asleep of Mary* [AD 400]

sinned, she would have never died. This also works the opposite way. If she did not die, she did not sin. Timothy of Jerusalem, an early Church writer, said this about Mary in AD 400: "Therefore the Virgin is immortal to this day, seeing that he who had dwelt in her transported her to the regions of her assumption."[152] Here, Saint Timothy is saying that Mary was assumed into Heaven and thus did not sin.

With Mary comes the Catholic Rosary. This is a problem for Protestants because of the repetitive prayer. Those who disagree with repetitive prayer will say that it's not divine to pray more than once, because God would hear us the first time.

The most notable verse from the Protestant side of the argument would be in the Gospel of Matthew when Jesus says, "Do not babble like the pagans with their many words."[153]

Jesus is not saying that repetitive prayer is evil. He's saying that babbling (talking fast and/or repetitively with little sense or meaning) is not divine.

Be that as it may, the Catholic Church doesn't even teach that the number of prayers in the rosary is what gives it merit. However, it is very hard to have a relationship with God when you do not talk to Him often.

Be that as it may, the Bible actually affirms that repetitive prayer is divine. In Matthew 26:44, Jesus prayed, "My Father, if it is not possible for this cup to be taken away unless I drink it, may your will be done" for a third time. This shows that repetitive prayer is good and worthy to God. The phrase "Pray without ceasing" is also found in two other biblical passages, Revelation 4:8 and 1 Thessalonians 5:17. In Revelation, John says, "Each of the four living creatures had six wings and was covered with eyes all around, even under its wings. Day and night they never stop saying: 'Holy, holy, holy is the Lord God Almighty, who was, and is, and is to come.'" In the first letter to the Thessalonians, Saint Paul says to "pray continuously." Repetitive prayer is not evil. The Bible is very clear about it.

---

[152] *Homily on Simeon and Anna* [AD 400]
[153] Matthew 6:7

Both Protestants and Catholics agree that Jesus was born of a virgin. However, the groups disagree on whether or not Mary continued to stay a virgin for her entire life. Before getting to arguments, it's important to note that Martin Luther, the father of the Reformation, referred to Mary as "everlasting virgin" in one of his letters.[154] So Protestants are going against the man who started their revolution in the first place. However, this does not necessarily prove that Mary was an everlasting virgin.

There are a couple of main arguments that Protestants use to argue that Mary was not a virgin for her entire life. Firstly, they will say that when Matthew says that Joseph did not consummate until she gave birth to a son.[155]

First and foremost, the word "until" does not necessarily mean a change. For example, when my mother says "stay out of trouble until you get back home," she is not insinuating that she wants me to get into trouble when I get home. However, even I will admit that it seems as if there was a subsequent change here. If one were to say "I did not have sex until I was married," the clear implication is that one's sex life changed after marriage.

However, the word for "until" in Greek (*heos*) could mean a few different things. Karlo Broussard points this out in his book *Meeting the Protestant Challenge*. Biblically, this word is used differently throughout. In the first letter to Timothy, Saint Paul says, "Until (*heos*) I come, devote yourself to the public reading of Scripture, to preaching and to teaching."[156] Needless to say, Saint Paul does not want Timothy to stop reading Scripture, preaching or teaching when he comes.

In his first letter to the Corinthians, Saint Paul says, "He will also keep you firm to (*heos*) the end, so that you will be blameless on the day of our Lord Jesus Christ."[157] Saint Paul undoubtedly is

---

[154] Taylor, Aaron, Nick Hallett, Francis Phillips, and Alexander Lucie-Smith, "Luther Affirmed Mary's Perpetual Virginity. It's a Shame That Many Protestants Now Reject It," Catholic Herald, January 6, 2017.

[155] Matthew 1:25

[156] 1 Timothy 4:13

[157] 1 Corinthians 1:8

not saying that Jesus leaves people after they die. Jesus Himself also makes a similar point in the Gospel of Matthew. "And surely I am with you always, to (*heos*) the very end of the age."[158]

It can be inferred that the Greek word *heos* does not always mean a subsequent change biblically speaking. In fact, Matthew even uses it to say "before" in his gospel: "When you are persecuted in one place, flee to another. Truly I tell you, you will not finish going through the towns of Israel before (*heos*) the Son of Man comes."[159] If Matthew uses *heos* in a different way here, who's to say that is not what he meant in 1:25? He certainly could've meant "Joseph knew her not before she bore." Moreover, even if he meant to reference the English world "until," that does not *always* constitute an ensuing change, as I've pointed out. This reality of language exists in biblical writings as well as day-to-day life. With that being said, it is impossible to indisputably say that Matthew was alluding to the English word "until" *and* that that word constitutes a successive change. We must look at other Bible verses to determine whether or not Mary was a virgin for her entire life.

Another argument that Protestants will make is that when the people in the synagogue heard Jesus preaching, they questioned, "Isn't this the carpenter's son? Isn't his mother's name Mary, and aren't his brothers James, Joseph, Simon and Judas? [56]Aren't all his sisters with us? Where then did this man get all these things?"[160]

Before talking about this verse, it's important to note that this is merely someone asking a question. These people are just now meeting Jesus, so asking if His brothers are James, Joseph, Simon, and Judas would not be out of the ordinary. Sort of like today when you meet someone for the first time and ask if that person has any siblings.

Of course, they could be speaking rhetorically, which is what I want to focus my attention on.

---

[158] Matthew 28:20
[159] Matthew 10:23
[160] Matthew 13:55–56

The Greek word for brother here is *adelfoß* (adelphos), which again could mean a multitude of different things. The different potential meanings are as follows:

1. A brother, whether born of the same two parents or only of the same father or mother
2. Having the same national ancestor, belonging to the same people, or countryman
3. Any fellow or man
4. A fellow believer, united to another by the bond of affection
5. An associate in employment or office
6. Brethren in Christ

   a. His brothers by blood
   b. All men
   c. Apostles
   d. Any Christian[161]

The word "adelphos" has a plethora of different meanings. If a Protestant were to say "I think the Jews in the synagogue meant biological brother," someone else could just say "I think they merely meant 'brethren in Christ,'" and the conversation would go nowhere without other Bible verses. Once more, unless one has a preconceived notion of what these verses are saying, there is no possible way to definitively say that Mary had other children.

A common, and argumentative, response to this would be "Every time the word 'adelphos' appears in the Bible, it translates to 'brother'. A rational person would assume that it means brother and not something else." That's a fair point. Let's say that it actually means "brother." There's still ambiguity. We don't know if it means biological brother or "brother in Christ" (which is a legitimate definition for the word, as I have shown above).

---

[161] Thayer and Smith, "Greek Lexicon entry for Adelphos," "The NAS New Testament Greek Lexicon," 1999.

Another common objection to this exegesis is that because Matthew talks about different family members, so the "brothers" mentioned above most likely is referring to brothers and not some other definition. Even if this were the case, it would be impossible to make the conclusion that they were Mary's kids. It's commonly known that Joseph was significantly older than Mary. Therefore, it would be disingenuous to throw out the idea that James, Joseph, Simon, and Judas were sons of Joseph from a different marriage. This would be acceptable from the second half of the first definition of the word.

Mary's perpetual virginity gets even more complex when looking at other verses such as Matthew 27:56 that Mary was the mother of James and Joseph. But which Mary is this? John's account of the crucifixion has Mary, wife of Clopas watching along with Jesus's mother.[162] Which Mary is Matthew talking about in chapter 27? There are different theories, but nonetheless, anyone being honest with himself will admit that scripture does not prove either side regarding the perpetual virginity.

All in all, you cannot say for certain that Mary had other kids from these verses. However, from a biblical standpoint, there aren't any verses that explicitly point to Mary's perpetual virginity. One of the most famous ones would be when Jesus is dying on the cross and he gives Mary to John as her son: "When Jesus saw his mother there, and the disciple whom he loved standing nearby, he said to her, 'Woman, here is your son.'"[163]

If John was Jesus's biological brother, this would make little sense. Why would Jesus remind Mary that John was her son while He was dying? Obviously, this is completely unnecessary. Furthermore, the verses above that talk about Jesus's "brothers" do not mention John.

Not even Protestants argue that John was the biological brother of Jesus. Why, then, did Jesus entrust Mary to John? If He had bio-

---

[162] John 19:25
[163] John 19:26

logical brothers, He would have entrusted her to them. (Needless to say, the alternative would be agitated younger siblings.)

With that being said, what did early Church Fathers say about this?

Here's a quote from an early Pope. In AD 450, Pope Leo I wrote, "His [Christ's] origin is different, but his [human] nature is the same. Human usage and custom were lacking, but by divine power a Virgin conceived, a Virgin bore, and Virgin she remained." Pope Leo insists that Mary stayed a virgin for her entire life.

Here's another quote from Cyril of Alexandria, an early doctor of the Church. He writes, "[T]he Word himself, coming into the Blessed Virgin herself, assumed for himself his own temple from the substance of the Virgin and came forth from her a man in all that could be externally discerned, while interiorly he was true God. Therefore he kept his Mother a virgin even after her childbearing." He is insisting that Mary stayed a virgin even after childbearing.

Here's the last quote from Leporius, an early Church philosopher in the year AD 426. He writes, "We confess, therefore, that our Lord and God, Jesus Christ, the only Son of God, born of the Father before the ages, and in times most recent, made man of the Holy Spirit and the ever-virgin Mary." He says that Christ was made man of the ever-virgin Mary. Meaning, she stayed a virgin for her entire life.

Saints

Mary is of course not the only saint that Catholics praise. Again, praising is not worshipping. We show respect to them because of what they did on Earth and for what they continue to do in Heaven.

From a nonbiblical perspective, we as a society show our veneration for certain individuals through the use of statues and relics. This of course is not a worshipping gesture. Bulls fans put a Michael Jordan statue outside the United Center not because they worship him, but because of the great things he did for that franchise.

This is the same philosophy Catholics have with saints. "But doesn't God disavow the making of graven images in the book of Exodus?"[164] someone may say. Yes, he did. However, "graven images" are something made for a worshipping gesture. Since Catholics do not worship these statues, it is not in violation of God's law.

To further illustrate my point, there are other examples of statues being built for various reasons. In fact, there's even an example later in the book of Exodus: "And make two cherubim out of hammered gold at the ends of the cover. Make one cherub on one end and the second cherub on the other; make the cherubim of one piece with the cover, at the two ends."[165] As seen by this verse, God is commanding Moses to make the Ark of the Covenant. The Israelites were not worshipping the angels that were on the ark.

A couple of books later in the book of Numbers, Moses makes a bronze serpent and puts it on a pole.[166] The prophet Jeremiah also describes a temple that Solomon built that had engraved angels,

---

[164] Exodus 20:4–5
[165] Exodus 25:18–19
[166] Numbers 21:8–9

trees, and flowers.[167] This temple also had bronze oxen, lions, and pomegranates.[168] They clearly did not worship these things in the Old Testament, so why is it a problem for Catholics to do the same thing? Having statues is not unbiblical. Moreover, from a common sense standpoint, having a statue or relic of someone you admire should be rather uncontroversial.

The response I usually get from this is, "While I can accept the idea of statues, I can't accept the idea that it is acceptable to pray to saints."

While prayer to saints is unanimously accepted until the reformation, there are a few Bible verses that Protestants will use to make this point. The first would be in the book of Deuteronomy where God is telling the Israelites not to practice necromancy.[169] It's worth noting that if a Catholic is practicing actual necromancy, that person is committing mortal sin. Necromancy is not merely communication with the dead. It is communication with the intent to gain information not known by those who are alive. Simply asking saints for prayers would not fall under this definition.

The next verse that they cite King Solomon is when he says that the dead know nothing.[170] First thing, this is not someone infallibly declaring what death is. Rather, he is trying to make sense of it from an earthly perspective. But even if he was right, there are a couple of reasons as to why this argument doesn't make sense for Protestants. Firstly, at the time of writing this, Heaven was not opened up yet. Catholics cannot pray to souls in Hell for prayers. This would be the only type of intercessory prayer to the dead that could've happened. So even if Solomon was saying definitively that people on Earth cannot ask for prayers of the dead, that could've changed after Jesus opened Heaven's gates with His sacrifice on the cross.

Moreover, there is not a single Christian that believes that when a person dies, that person knows "nothing." If your soul is in Hell, you know that you do not want to be there. If your soul is in Heaven,

---

[167] 1 Kings 6:23–29
[168] 1 Kings 7:25–45
[169] Deuteronomy 18:10–11
[170] Ecclesiastes 9:5

you know you are with God and that this is a place of eternal happiness. If the dead truly know nothing, then there is no afterlife. Since the idea of someone knowing "nothing" after they die is unbiblical, why is it controversial for Catholics to say that saints know more than nothing?

However, the most used verse from the Protestant argument is that Saint Paul says there is one mediator between God and man— the Lord Jesus Christ.[171] The implication here is that intercessory prayer is evil because it requires a mediator.

Anyone who uses this verse to say that intercessory prayer is evil is being a fool. I can guarantee that everyone who uses this verse as an argument against intercessory prayer has either prayed for someone on their behalf or asked someone else to pray for them. Saint Paul obviously is not talking about all types of mediation. Why is it that mediation for people on Earth is acceptable, but mediation with those in Heaven with God is not? Additionally, Saint Paul tells the Romans that death cannot separate us from the love of God.[172] Saint Paul is merely saying that Christ's mediation is unique, not that all types of mediation are unacceptable. If that were the case, the Bible verses that talk about intercessory prayer need to be thrown out.[173] We also have biblical evidence that God can provide others in Heaven with prayer requests from Earth. This is seen in the book of Revelations when an angel gives prayers of the people to God.[174]

We also see Jesus talking to dead Moses and Elijah in Matthew's gospel.[175] This alone makes clear that talking to the dead is not inherently sinful. I have heard some objections to this, most notably that "it's different for Jesus." How so? Yes, Jesus is God, but He is also fully man. Was it sinful for Jesus to talk to the dead? If so, then Jesus could not have been God because God cannot sin. If it was not sinful, why would it be sinful for us? The exegesis just doesn't make sense.

---

[171] 1 Timothy 2:5

[172] Romans 8:35–39

[173] Romans 15:30, Colossians 4;3, 1 Thessalonians 5:25, 2 Thessalonians 1:11 2 Thessalonians 3:1, Ephesians 6:18–19

[174] Revelations 5:8

[175] Matthew 17:3

Here, Methodius is praying to Mary.

Here's a short quote written in AD 393 from Ambrose of Milan, an early Church writer. "May Peter, who wept so efficaciously for himself, weep for us and turn towards us Christ's benign countenance." Here, the writer is asking Peter to weep for us and turn toward Christ for us, as a remission of our sins.

Here's the last quote, from Saint Jerome, written in the year AD 406:

> You say in your book that while we live we are able to pray for each other, but afterwards when we have died, the prayer of no person for another can be heard... But if the apostles and martyrs while still in the body can pray for others, at a time when they ought still be solicitous about themselves, how much more will they do so after their crowns, victories, and triumphs?

Saint Jerome insists that those in Heaven pray for us on Earth. Why, then, do Protestants believe that those in Heaven do not pray for us? Or better yet, why do they believe we should not ask for those prayers?

Once Saved Doesn't Mean Always Saved

One of the most important philosophies in Christian theology is how we are saved. This should be studied heavily, because if we are wrong, it could mean eternity in Hell. Studying and prophesying the correct philosophy regarding salvation would save a multitude of souls.

Throughout this paragraph, note that a Sola Fide (as the reformers knew it) and eternal security were both unanimously rejected in the early church. Along with this, praying for the dead, and in extension Purgatory, is unanimously accepted as well.

It's important to point out that just because a verse says that faith is required for salvation, that does not necessarily mean that faith is exclusive. For instance, if a professor told his students that they need a specific calculator for the class, it would not mean that the calculator is the only thing necessary for the class. More than likely, the student would need to purchase/rent a textbook, and take notes somehow.

So when Saint Paul says that the righteous are saved through faith,[176] it is impossible to say that he means faith alone without referencing other Bible verses. It would make sense, therefore, to look at other Bible verses for evidence. There are other verses as well that say that one needs faith, contrary to something else, in order to be saved. Again, these verses never say faith is exclusive. They solely say that faith is necessary, but not something else. To go back to the professor example, if the professor says, "You will need this specific calculator for this class, but you do not need a specific kind of writing utensil," to reiterate, the professor is not saying that the calculator is the only

---

[176] Romans 1:17

thing necessary for his class. Moreover, this does not mean that every type of utensil is unnecessary. It just means that one specific kind is not necessary. (For example's sake, let's assume that the students were originally using this utensil because they thought it was obligatory to receive an *A* in the class.)

This analogy can be applied to the Bible as well. So when Saint Paul says that the righteous need faith and not works of the law, it does not mean that faith is the only thing necessary for salvation. Furthermore, it does not mean that all works are unnecessary. Likewise, saying works "of the law" are not necessary for salvation would not be the same as saying all works are unnecessary for salvation. Much like saying a specific kind of writing utensil is unnecessary does not mean that all writing utensils are unnecessary.

All these verses involve Saint Paul speaking to specific groups of people in an attempt to get those groups to become Christians. He is saying that they are saved through faith (not faith alone), rather than works of the law.

The issue, and the reason it's imperative that we study these verses, is that works "of the law" are not the same as actions. Works "of the law" refers to the Jews coming out of Egypt, the Torah. Saint Paul is saying that the righteous are saved through faith (not faith alone), and not of the law with which the Israelites were forced to obey. Another thing to mention, a great portion of these verses that Protestants will cite were written by Saint Paul. There's nothing intrinsically wrong with quoting him. However, it's important that we know this. Quoting the same person has its issues, one being that a person could have a specific way of talking that is different from others. For instance, Saint Paul mentions that works "of the law" are not required for entrance to Heaven. Thus, afterward, when Saint Paul mentions works not being required, it can be assumed that he means works of the law. It's implied that he's only omitting the prepositional phrase here and not speaking of a different thing. If he were, it would be made very clear. Like previously stated, an omniscient being would not be unclear as to how to achieve salvation. If Saint Paul was talking about actions and not "works of the law," he would have made it astonishingly obvious. Not only that, but we know that

Saint Paul did not say that works are irrelevant to salvation, as he says so in his letter to the Romans: "God will repay each person according to what they have done."[177]

I also must make some distinctions about the Catholic view of "faith and works" before moving on. The Church teaches that we are saved through faith, Baptism, and the observance of the Commandments." (footnote CCC 2068) Works are not necessary for initial justification. Once one is in the state of justification, only then can works justify them.

We are saved through grace alone and can bring nothing to it, it is a free gift from God. Once we are in the state of grace, we can increase justification (become more righteous). This is exactly what happened to Phinehas in Psalm 106:30-31. Phinehas, while in the state of grace, was credited righteous for endless generations. These verses are extremely powerful because even if a Protestant were to say that James is talking about justification before men in chapter 2, they cannot possibly say that for Phinehas. How can human beings credit someone as righteous (a legal declaration) for endless generations? If this verse was talking about justification before men, it would say something along the lines of "Phinehas was considered righteous by many generations to come." In order to get this interpretation, Protestants have to read this into the text.

To simplify, allow me to give a specific example. If an atheist gave a million dollars to charity, it only counts as natural good. It counts as nothing to God. Take this same atheist, Baptized and in the state of grace, who sees a homeless man on the street. He only has one dollar in his pocket. He gives the dollar to the homeless man. That one dollar (because he is in the state of grace) counts towards his justification and allows him to become closer to God. Everything done by grace alone, from initial justification to final sanctification, is a gift from God, and a heresy to say otherwise.

Sidenote-This is why other interpretations of Paul do not pose a problem for Catholics. When Paul separates faith from works and says that the faith is counted as righteous, we do not have an issue,

---

[177] Romans 2:6

as we are considered righteous at initial justification. Likewise, when Paul separates works from grace, and says that those works are not meritorious, we do not have an issue, since works not done in grace are not meritorious.

"But John says that we can know we are saved if we believe,"[178] a Protestant will respond. Keep in mind that the word "know" has different meanings. I could definitely know that the pen next to me is gray. This is something that can be proven and is precise.

Take this example and compare it to me saying, "I just know that the Republicans will win the election this November." I cannot prove this. (Until, of course, November comes around.) Nonetheless, there are two definitions of the word "know." Because of this, Protestants cannot determine what John meant without using the words "I think" and "probably." Their subjective view of what the Bible is does not supersede what John really meant. The Bible also says that those who believe are saved. (See Romans 1:16 and Mark 16:16). This is still not an argument for eternal security. These verses do not specify what we must believe. "We must believe that Jesus was God." Yes and no. We must believe that Jesus was God, but it doesn't stop there. Even if someone believes that Jesus was God, they are not saved if they are pro choice for example. So these verses indicate that we must not only believe that the Son of God died for us on the cross but we must believe the entire word of God. This includes the written and unwritten form and the other verses that say we must do x, y, and z in other to be saved (other than faith).

Protestants tend to combat these verses by saying that while faith alone is what saves, faith always creates action. If there is no action, there is no faith. First and foremost, to even make this argument, the Protestant would have to concede that there is some type of action involved in salvation. Without action, there is no salvation. "Loving Jesus is the only thing that is necessary," they will say. Even if that were true, you'd have to explain how one would go about loving Jesus. Jesus mentions a couple of times in the gospel that if

---

[178] 1 John 5:13

we love Him[179] and wish to enter eternal life,[180] we must keep His commandments. Even if the philosophy of "we only need to love Jesus!" is accurate from a biblical standpoint, you would still have to keep His commandments in order to show that you truly love Him.

There are a couple of other verses that Protestants will cite that appear to teach eternal security. There are some Bible verses that say a group of people have (past tense) been saved. The most famous of which would be Ephesians 2:8–9.

These verses are the most well-known because Paul says that the Ephesians were originally not saved through works.

As I previously stated, when Paul says "works," he more than likely means works of the law. A Protestant could say "he meant all action," and I could say "he only meant works of the law." Because we cannot definitively determine what Paul meant without outside Bible verses, Protestants using this verse and saying "he meant all works" only makes sense with a preconceived notion of what the Bible means.

However, Paul is most likely talking about action here. With that being said, even if Paul meant "any action," it does not negate the Catholic view of salvation. The initial salvation that I received at Baptism was not because of anything I did, but the faith of my mother. Just because the initial salvation that I received was not based on action does not mean that getting that salvation back does not require action. It is also worth noting that the Catholic Church teaches that we do nothing in our own power to gain the grace sufficient for salvation, so that's another possible exegesis. This verse can be looked at a variety of different ways, none of which argue for eternal security. Even if the Ephesians were saved through faith and not action originally, it does not mean that they will keep that salvation forever. That simply isn't in the text.

Take this analogy for example. I just got a special, man-made crucifix for Christmas from my grandparents. I did not earn it

---

179 John 14:15
180 Matthew 19:16–17

through action, but the love of my grandparents. If I lose the crucifix, I have to engage in some kind of action to get it back.

Continuing with this ideal of eternal security, just because someone was saved in a past experience does not mean that that person can't lose salvation at a later date. If I save my little cousin from getting run over by a car by getting her out of the way, that does not prevent her from going back into the road, thus needing salvation again.

An argument against this would be that the author says that we are sanctified "once and for all" in the book of Hebrews.[181] However, this verse cannot possibly mean that all sins, past, present, and future, are forgiven. If that were the case, people would not have to seek a relationship with God in order to be saved. After all, if Jesus saved everyone on the cross, Protestant and Catholic theology would be disavowed. After all, both groups affirm that faith in God and repentance of sin is necessary for salvation.

We see several scriptural examples warning us not to leave God. John 15:6 and Hebrews 3:12 are just a couple of examples of this. If the eternal security crowd is correct in saying that those who are once saved cannot lose that salvation, then why would God warn us? That would be like warning someone not to fly a plane a certain way if they do not have a pilot's license. They can't fly, so there's no reason to be warning them. The same analogy applies. If we are eternally secure, there would be no reason for these warning passages.

"If they fall away, they never had that salvation to begin with. They weren't real Christians. Look at 1 John 2:19! There are a few issues with that line of reasoning:

1. How can you fall away from something you never had? That would be like saying you can fall off a tree without even climbing it.
2. No one denies that there are fake Christians. However, it a gross generalization to claim that because John talks about

---

[181] Hebrews 10:10–14

fake Christians, every person who leaves the Church was faking it the entire time.

3. Continuing with the previous point, it creates very unusual and frankly ridiculous scenarios for people who believe this. Imagine someone who reads the Bible every day, goes to church twice a week, goes to Bible camp, spends money to go to seminary, then leaves the Church. Was this person faking it the entire time? The logical answer is no. They were not faking it but merely left the Church. But because of their extreme confirmation bias, those who believe in eternal security can't admit that this person lost their salvation. So they must reach the illogical conclusion that this person who devoted much of their life to a specific cause was faking it the entire time.

4. If this person was not a "true Christian," how can anyone call themselves a Christian? No one has infallible knowledge of the future. Therefore, if Christianity is based on whether or not you will leave it in the future, Christianity cannot possibly exist in the present tense. You could only say that someone "was" a Christian after they died.

Going along with this idea, it's important to note that Saint Paul teaches that one may fall away from God even though they think they are secure.[182] He also mentions that one must remain in the kindness of God if they do not want to be cut off.[183]

We also see early Church Fathers talking about rewards and merits for people after they did something (not merely because they believed in God).

Here's a quote from Justin Martyr, an early saint, on the topic of faith and good deeds. He writes,

> We have learned from the prophets and we hold
> it as true that punishments and chastisements

---

[182] 1 Corinthians 10:11–12
[183] Romans 11:22

and good rewards are distributed according to the merit of each man's actions. Were this not the case, and were all things to happen according to the decree of fate, there would be nothing at all in our power. If fate decrees that this man is to be good and that one wicked, then neither is the former to be praised nor the latter to be blamed.

So if men can be wicked, those must be the men who don't do good deeds. Of course, this could always mean that those who are "wicked" are simply men who do not want to be with God, and therefore will be "blamed," but what does this mean? Let's look at other quotes to see what others thought made a man "wicked."

Here's another quote from Tatian the Syrian, an early philosopher. In AD 170, he wrote, "[T]he wicked man is justly punished, having become depraved of himself; and the just man is worthy of praise for his honest deeds, since it was in his free choice that he did not transgress the will of God."

The wicked man, meaning a man who sins, is justly punished. Could this mean that only those who do not believe in God are considered wicked? There's always that possibility. However, in this quote, Tatian also says "in his free choice that he did not transgress the will of God." Meaning that this person knew the will of God and chose to ignore it. This made him a wicked man.

Here's a quote from Hippolytus, another early philosopher. In AD 212, he wrote,

> Standing before [Christ's] judgment, all of them, men, angels, and demons, crying out in one voice, shall say: "Just is your judgment," and the justice of that cry will be apparent in the recompense made to each. To those who have done well, everlasting enjoyment shall be given; while to lovers of evil shall be given eternal punishment.

Again, he is reiterating that you can't just believe God to go to Heaven. You must also not be a lover of sin.

The Bible says that nothing unclean can ever enter Heaven.[184] It can be inferred that this means that those with sin cannot enter Heaven. It's also said that we are still sinning and are attached to sin, even at the end of our earthly lives.[185] Since you do not get into Heaven simply by believing in God, there should be a purification after death. After all, the only alternate reality would be that anyone with sin on his soul at the time of death goes to Hell. Went to Church and prayed every day but stole a pencil right before you died? Sorry, you're spending eternity in Hell! Certainly, a loving God would not have these two options: either you are perfect until your time of death or you will burn forever in Hell.

Why, then, would we be able to go straight to Heaven after we die? After all, if Satan got kicked out of Heaven for sin, what makes Protestants think they can get into Heaven with sin? Protestants will argue that Purgatory isn't a true way of thinking about God because "it isn't in the Bible" and "it nullifies the sacrifice of Jesus on the cross." As I already explained earlier, Jesus's sacrifice on the cross does not allow everyone who believes in Him go to Heaven with no exception. Eternal security is a made-up doctrine.

When Protestants argue that Purgatory is not in the Bible, there are two ways in which they go about it. They will either say, "The word 'Purgatory' is not in the Bible, therefore the concept is unbiblical." Most Protestant theology is rather ridiculous. However, this one may take the cake. Just because a word is not specifically said in the Bible does not mean the concept is not there. The most common instance regarding this in the Bible is the word "trinity." The word "trinity" is not explicitly stated in the Bible, but the reference to it is clear. The specific word has no importance.

They could also say that the concept of Purgatory (or praying for the dead) is not biblical. That is also wrong, but it's much more complicated.

---

[184] Revelation 21:27
[185] 1 John 1:8

First, the concept of praying for sins so that they may be loose is clearly referenced in Maccabees, but Martin Luther took that book out. Maccabees says, "For if he had not hoped that they that were slain should rise again, it would have seemed superfluous and vain to pray for the dead. And because he considered that they who had fallen asleep with godliness, had great grace laid up for them. It is therefore a holy and wholesome thought to pray for the dead, that they may be loosed from sins." As seen by this verse, it is holy to pray for the dead souls in Purgatory so that they may be released from their sins.

Protestants will always combat this verse by saying, "Well, that book isn't inspired. You need to prove the existence of Purgatory from my sixty-six books." Up front, this argument sounds unusual. I already argued that these books were inspired. Even so, why in the world would I agree to those terms? That would be like a Muslim going up to me and saying, "Prove to me that Jesus was the Messiah using only the Koran."

Be that as it may, there are other references to Purgatory in the Bible as well. First, Jesus preaches to the "spirits in prison."[186] Who could this be? It couldn't be Heaven, because those in Heaven are not in a prison. It also could not be Hell, because preaching in Hell would not make any sense. They are there forever. Why bother preaching? Furthermore, the Greek word *phylake* does not mean Hell. The Greek word *hadou* translates to Hell in English. Peter doesn't use that; he uses *phylake*. Why do this? After all, when Jesus tells Peter that he is the rock upon which He will build His Church, he says, "The gates of Hell (hadou) shall not prevail against it." Why be ambiguous with the word when he could have just said *hadou*?

Paul also prays for his dead friend, Onesiphorus, in the second letter of Timothy:

> May the Lord show mercy to the household of Onesiphorus, because he often refreshed me and was not ashamed of my chains. On the contrary,

---

[186] 1 Peter 3:19

when he was in Rome, he searched hard for me
until he found me. May the Lord grant that he
will find mercy from the Lord on that day! You
know very well in how many ways he helped me
in Ephesus.[187]

In this verse, Paul prays for his friend to God so that he may be
loosened from sin. Some Protestants try to defend this, by saying that
Onesiphorus either wasn't dead when Paul was praying. However,
J. N. D. Kelly admits that Onesiphorus was dead in this verse in *A
Commentary on the Pastoral Epistles*:

> On the assumption, which must be correct, that
> Onesiphorus was dead when the words were writ-
> ten, we have here an example, unique in the N.T.,
> of Christian prayer for the departed… the com-
> mendation of the dead man to the divine mercy.
> There is nothing surprising in Paul's use of such
> a prayer, for intercession for the dead had been
> sanctioned in Pharisaic circles at any rate since
> the date of 2 Macc 12:43–45. Inscriptions in the
> Roman catacombs and elsewhere prove that the
> practice established itself among Christians from
> very early times.

Other prominent Protestant historians have also admitted
that Paul was praying for a dead man. These include, but are not
limited to, Philip Schaff, Alfred Plummer, James Maurice Wilson,
Sydney Charles Gayford, John Henry Bernard, Charles John Ellicott,
William Barclay, Henry Alford, and W. Robertson Nicoll.[188]

Why would Paul do this? If Paul knew his friend was in Heaven
or Hell, he wouldn't bother praying for them because there would
be no reason to do so. They are at their destination, and there is

---

[187] 2 Timothy 1:16–18
[188] St. Paul Prayed for Onesiphorus, Who Was Dead. (n.d.). Retrieved May 10, 2020.

no changing it. The only reason Paul would pray for Onesiphorus would be to pray him out of Purgatory. There is no logical explanation for anything else.

We see Paul describe Purgatory in his first letter to the Corinthians. He writes, "If it is burned up, the builder will suffer loss but yet will be saved—even though only as one escaping through the flames."[189] Paul is saying here that someone will be saved but they have to escape flames (Purgatory).

Despite the Protestant assertion, life with God does not mean that those will be with Him as soon as they die. When I get off work, it takes about twenty minutes for me to get home. Much like the path to God, there is a step in between. Contrary to what Protestants will say, Purgatory is biblical.

That being said, what did the early Church Fathers say about Purgatory?

Here's a quote from Abercius, an early philosophical writer:

> The citizen of a prominent city, I erected this while I lived, that I might have a resting place for my body. Abercius is my name, a disciple of the chaste Shepherd who feeds his sheep on the mountains and in the fields, who has great eyes surveying everywhere, who taught me the faithful writings of life. Standing by, I, Abercius, ordered this to be inscribed: Truly, I was in my seventy-second year. May everyone who is in accord with this and who understands it pray for Abercius.

Protestants will argue that Abercius here is only talking about prayer for himself while he is alive. However, this is likely inaccurate, as earlier in the quote, he says, "I might have a resting place for my body." Meaning, he was referring to his death. He wanted people to pray for him after his death. Why else would he want this unless he

---

[189] 1 Corinthians 3:15

was in Purgatory? There would be no reason to do this if he was in Heaven or Hell.

Here's another quote from Tertullan, who was referenced earlier in the chapter. In AD 216, he wrote: "A woman, after the death of her husband...prays for his soul and asks that he may, while waiting, find rest; and that he may share in the first resurrection. And each year, on the anniversary of his death, she offers the sacrifice." Again I reiterate, why would she pray for a soul in Heaven or Hell? There's no need to do so. They're at their destination. They either don't need prayers if they are in Heaven, or it wouldn't help them anyway in Hell.

Here's another quote written in AD 392 by John Chrysostom. Again. Chrysostom was referenced earlier in a different quote. He writes, "Let us help and commemorate them. If Job's sons were purified by their father's sacrifice [Job 1:5], why would we doubt that our offerings for the dead bring them some consolation? Let us not hesitate to help those who have died and to offer our prayers for them." Again I say to you, why would they pray for the dead if Purgatory was nonexistent? They never say the word "Purgatory," but that does not mean it does not exist.

To summarize the above, the idea that once you are saved, you will always be saved is an unbiblical idea. Protestants only believe this because it's a profoundly effortless philosophy. The only backing their credo has comes from Protestants with an overwhelming confirmation bias who do not want to admit that their ideology of "I don't have to do anything; I know I am going to Heaven because I believe in God" is not biblical or historic.

Becoming a Better Catholic

The philosophies of the Catholic Church can all be summarized by one sentence: spread the gospel. Now, I'm sure you have heard this statement hundreds of times. "Spread the gospel" is a term said regularly among Christians. But how, dear reader, are you going to do this? You may be thinking, "I don't really like talking about God in front of friends." I didn't ask you to do that. What I asked you to do is to spread the Gospel. This can be with words or actions. As Saint Francis of Assisi famously said, "Spread the Gospel at all times, use words only when necessary."

Here are some ways you can spread the gospel without saying a word. When you volunteer at a food pantry, help people move, or even do something as simple as holding a door open for someone, you're spreading the gospel. You are, after all, defined by actions and not by faith alone.

Another thing that can be very easily done is to realize that you do not know everyone's story. What I mean by that is this—Say you work in retail, and a customer just came up to you and was basically a huge jerk. You were doing your best, but they kept calling you names and yelling at you for going too slow. What's the immediate reaction to this? "That person is a jerk" or "that person isn't nice." However, I would encourage you to stop doing this.

Imagine this same scenario, but the person yelling at you just lost their entire family in a car crash. While this reality is very often not the case, it's a good tool to use. It's like people in AA pretending everyone they come across is trying their best to stay sober all day and will be irritable because of it. You can imagine any terrible scenario you'd like. One of them may even be true. "That person was abused" or "That person just learned they have cancer." There's a multitude of different hypothetical circumstances that could be said to oneself. You don't know everyone's story, so don't act as if you do. No one is a jerk for no reason—always remember that.

I'd also like you to always remember that Jesus thought of everyone when he died on the cross. He didn't just think of your friends, He didn't just think of your family, but also, He thought of the person you claim to hate as well. For a visual, imagine that Jesus is about to carry his cross, looks at you, and says, "You're worth it." This is a very powerful thought. Jesus would do this for any one of us, not just one or two people. He would have died on the cross to save the sins of even one person.

To put this into perspective, imagine you, like God, have omnipotent power. Like God, you can snap your fingers and create anything. I'm not sure what you'd create, but I'd snap my fingers and create a really nice house, a really nice car, and other things that are going to make my life more enjoyable.

Now imagine I do that, then I'm hungry. So for lunch, I snap my fingers and create a rotten apple to eat. Obviously, I would never do this. I can create anything, and I choose to create this junk? No one would ever do this. A being that knows everything would not either. An omnipotent being would also know what is trash and what is not. Reader, you are good enough for a being that knows everything. Why aren't you good enough for yourself?

I very much enjoy these thought experiments, because it helps those who do not understand God to better understand Him. So, I have another one. Let's say for example's sake you have a friend who can tell the future. If you have a decision to make, you can ask him, and he will tell you the one that will ultimately make you the happiest.

Now imagine you have a very tough decision to make. You could go to your friend, but you go, "Sorry man, I can do this myself." Why would anyone do this? Ask him! He's right there! I imagine this is how God feels sometimes. Ask him, reader. He will give you the answer you are looking for, even if it's the unpopular one.

Going forth, I would encourage you to make your God bigger so your worries can become lesser. What usually happens when I tell people to put God first is they say, "Okay, okay, but he has to go under school and work and family and friends and…" Then, God is fifth on the list and hardly a priority. I understand that you have other priorities. But when you put God first, everything else lines up. Putting God first in your life will set everything else into place and make you a happier person overall. When you make your God bigger, your worries become lesser. Instead of focusing on the worries, focus on God.

Focusing on another point here, imagine you are a bodybuilder. Think of a comparison of the results of someone who works out six days a week compared to someone who only works out one day a week. Probably a pretty massive difference in results, right? Ladies and gentlemen, it's the same thing as with God. If you only go to Mass on Sundays and don't pray to God any other day of the week, your spiritual life will not be nearly as strong as someone who prays daily. Like previously stated, keep God number one, and everything else will sort itself out.

Concluding Words

Finding the true religion of God may not be as hard as it seems. Catholic beliefs are both biblical and historic. When Protestants and other groups argue that our theology is not biblical, they are wrong. Catholic theology is biblical; it just isn't biblical through their own abstract view of what they want the Bible to say.

About the Author

Parker Manning is a nineteen-year-old Catholic apologist who wants others to learn about the one true faith through his writing. Parker is currently studying to be an economics professor. This is his first book, but he has more coming along the way.

Lightning Source UK Ltd.
Milton Keynes UK
UKHW040707160223
417122UK00001B/190